Workshop on Cognitive Aspects of Computational Language Learning

(CogACLL 2014)

Held at the 14th Conference of the European Chapter of the Association for Computational Linguistics

Gothenburg, Sweden
26 April 2014

ISBN: 978-1-63266-400-6

Printed from e-media with permission by:

Curran Associates, Inc.
57 Morehouse Lane
Red Hook, NY 12571

proceedings.com

Some format issues inherent in the e-media version may also appear in this print version.

Printed by Curran Associates, Inc. (2014)

For permission requests, please contact the Association for Computational Linguistics at the address below.

Association for Computational Linguistics
209 N. Eighth Street
Stroudsburg, Pennsylvania 18360

Phone: 1-570-476-8006
Fax: 1-570-476-0860

acl@aclweb.org

Additional copies of this publication are available from:

Curran Associates, Inc.
57 Morehouse Lane
Red Hook, NY 12571 USA
Phone: 845-758-0400
Fax: 845-758-2634
Email: curran@proceedings.com
Web: www.proceedings.com

Introduction

The Workshop on Cognitive Aspects of Computational Language Learning (CogACLL) took place on April 26, 2014 in Gothenburg, Sweden, in conjunction with the 14th Conference of the European Chapter of the Association for Computational Linguistics. The workshop was endorsed by ACL Special Interest Group on Natural Language Learning (SIGNLL). This is the fifth edition of related workshops that was first held at ACL 2007 in Prague, EACL 2009 in Athens, EACL 2012 in Avignon and as a standalone event in Paris 2013.

The workshop is targeted at anyone interested in the relevance of computational techniques for understanding first, second and bilingual language acquisition and change or loss in normal and pathological conditions.

The human ability to acquire and process language has long attracted interest and generated much debate due to the apparent ease with which such a complex and dynamic system is learnt and used on the face of ambiguity, noise and uncertainty. This subject raises many questions ranging from the nature vs. nurture debate of how much needs to be innate and how much needs to be learned for acquisition to be successful, to the mechanisms involved in this process (general vs specific) and their representations in the human brain. There are also developmental issues related to the different stages consistently found during acquisition (e.g. one word vs. two words) and possible organizations of this knowledge. These have been discussed in the context of first and second language acquisition and bilingualism, with cross linguistic studies shedding light on the influence of the language and the environment.

The past decades have seen a massive expansion in the application of statistical and machine learning methods to natural language processing (NLP). This work has yielded impressive results in numerous speech and language processing tasks, including e.g. speech recognition, morphological analysis, parsing, lexical acquisition, semantic interpretation, and dialogue management. The good results have generally been viewed as engineering achievements. Recently researchers have begun to investigate the relevance of computational learning methods for research on human language acquisition and change. The use of computational modeling is a relatively recent trend boosted by advances in machine learning techniques, and the availability of resources like corpora of child and child-directed sentences, and data from psycholinguistic tasks by normal and pathological groups. Many of the existing computational models attempt to study language tasks under cognitively plausible criteria (such as memory and processing limitations that humans face), and to explain the developmental stages observed in the acquisition and evolution of the language abilities. In doing so, computational modeling provides insight into the plausible mechanisms involved in human language processes, and inspires the development of better language models and techniques. These investigations are very important since if computational techniques can be used to improve our understanding of human language acquisition and change, these will not only benefit cognitive sciences in general but will reflect back to NLP and place us in a better position to develop useful language models.

We invited submissions on relevant topics, including:

- Computational learning theory and analysis of language learning and organization
- Computational models of first, second and bilingual language acquisition
- Computational models of language changes in clinical conditions
- Computational models and analysis of factors that influence language acquisition and use in different age groups and cultures

- Computational models of various aspects of language and their interaction effect in acquisition, processing and change
- Computational models of the evolution of language
- Data resources and tools for investigating computational models of human language processes
- Empirical and theoretical comparisons of the learning environment and its impact on language processes
- Cognitively oriented Bayesian models of language processes
- Computational methods for acquiring various linguistic information (related to e.g. speech, morphology, lexicon, syntax, semantics, and discourse) and their relevance to research on human language acquisition
- Investigations and comparisons of supervised, unsupervised and weakly-supervised methods for learning (e.g. machine learning, statistical, symbolic, biologically-inspired, active learning, various hybrid models) from a cognitive perspective.

Submissions included works on specific languages like English, Portuguese and German, along with crosslinguistic studies. Besides paper presentations the technical program included two invited talks by Philippe Blache, from Aix-Marseille Université and CNRS (France) and Alexander Clark, from King's College London (UK).

Acknowledgements
We would like to thank the members of the Program Committee for the timely reviews and the authors for their valuable contributions. Thierry Poibeau is partly funded by TransferS (laboratoire d'excellence, program "Investissements d'avenir" ANR-10-IDEX-0001-02 PSL* and ANR-10-LABX-0099); Aline Villavicencio by projects CNPq 482520/2012-4, 478222/2011-4, 312184/2012-3 and 551964/2011-1; Muntsa Padró by project CAPES PNPD-2484/2009.

Alessandro Lenci
Muntsa Padró
Thierry Poibeau
Aline Villavicencio

Workshop Chairs:

Alessandro Lenci, University of Pisa (Italy)
Muntsa Padró, Federal University of Rio Grande do Sul (Brazil)
Thierry Poibeau, LATTICE-CNRS (France)
Aline Villavicencio, Federal University of Rio Grande do Sul (Brazil)

Invited Speakers:

Philippe Blache, Aix-Marseille Université and CNRS (France)
Alexander Clark, King's College, London (UK)

Program Committee:

Afra Alishahi, Tilburg University (Netherlands)
Colin J Bannard, University of Texas at Austin (USA)
Marco Baroni, University of Trento (Italy)
Robert Berwick, Massachusetts Institute of Technology (USA)
Philippe Blache, Aix-Marseille Université and CNRS (France)
Jim Blevins, University of Cambridge (UK)
Antal van den Bosch, Radboud University Nijmegen (Netherlands)
Chris Brew, Nuance Communications (USA)
Ted Briscoe, University of Cambridge (UK)
Alexander Clark, Royal Holloway, University of London (UK)
Robin Clark, University of Pennsylvania (USA)
Stephen Clark, University of Cambridge (UK)
Matthew W. Crocker, Saarland University (Germany)
Walter Daelemans, University of Antwerp (Belgium)
Dan Dediu, Max Planck Institute for Psycholinguistics (The Netherlands)
Barry Devereux, University of Cambridge (UK)
Benjamin Fagard, Lattice-CNRS (France)
Jeroen Geertzen, University of Cambridge (UK)
Ted Gibson, Massachusetts Institute of Technology (USA)
Henriette Hendriks, University of Cambridge (UK)
Marco Idiart, Federal University of Rio Grande do Sul (Brazil)
Mark Johnson, Macquarie University (Australia)
Aravind Joshi, University of Pennsylvania (USA)
Gianluca Lebani, University of Pisa (Italy)
Igor Malioutov, Massachusetts Institute of Technology (USA)
Marie-Catherine de Marneffe, The Ohio State University (USA)
Maria Alice de Mattos Pimenta, Federal University of ABC (Brazil)
Maria Alice Parente, Federal University of Rio Grande do Sul (Brazil)
Massimo Poesio, University of Trento (Italy)
Brechtje Post, University of Cambridge (UK)
Ari Rappoport, The Hebrew University of Jerusalem (Israel)
Anne Reboul, L2C2-CNRS (France)
Kenji Sagae, University of Southern California (USA)
Sabine Schulte im Walde, University of Stuttgart (Germany)
Ekaterina Shutova, University of California, Berkeley (USA)
Maity Siqueira, Federal University of Rio Grande do Sul (Brazil)
Mark Steedman, University of Edinburgh (UK)

Suzanne Stevenson, University of Toronto (Canada)
Remi van Trijp, Sony Computer Science Laboratory Paris (France)
Shuly Wintner, University of Haifa (Israel)
Charles Yang, University of Pennsylvania (USA)
Beracah Yankama, Massachusetts Institute of Technology (USA)
Menno van Zaanen, Tilburg University (Netherlands)
Alessandra Zarcone, University of Stuttgart (Germany)

Table of Contents

Challenging incrementality in human language processing: two operations for a cognitive architecture
Philippe Blache 1

A Brazilian Portuguese Phonological-prosodic Algorithm Applied to Language Acquisition: A Case Study
Vera Vasilévski, Márcio José Araujo and Helena Ferro Blasi 3

Bayesian inference as a cross-linguistic word segmentation strategy: Always learning useful things
Lawrence Phillips and Lisa Pearl 9

Learning the hyperparameters to learn morphology
Stella Frank 14

An explicit statistical model of learning lexical segmentation using multiple cues
Çağrı Çöltekin and John Nerbonne 19

Distributional Learning as a Theory of Language Acquisition
Alexander Clark 29

A multimodal corpus for the evaluation of computational models for (grounded) language acquisition
Judith Gaspers, Maximilian Panzner, Andre Lemme, Philipp Cimiano, Katharina J. Rohlfing and Sebastian Wrede 30

Towards a computational model of grammaticalization and lexical diversity
Christian Bentz and Paula Buttery 38

How well can a corpus-derived co-occurrence network simulate human associative behavior?
Gemma Bel Enguix, Reinhard Rapp and Michael Zock 43

Agent-based modeling of language evolution
Torvald Lekvam, Björn Gambäck and Lars Bungum 49

Missing Generalizations: A Supervised Machine Learning Approach to L2 Written Production
Daniel Wiechmann and Elma Kerz 55

Conference Program

Saturday April 26, 2014

9:30 Opening and Introduction

Invited Talk 1

9:40 *Challenging incrementality in human language processing: two operations for a cognitive architecture*
Philippe Blache

10:30 Coffee Break

Session 1: Phonology, morphology and word segmentation

11:00 *A Brazilian Portuguese Phonological-prosodic Algorithm Applied to Language Acquisition: A Case Study*
Vera Vasilévski, Márcio José Araujo and Helena Ferro Blasi

11:20 *Bayesian inference as a cross-linguistic word segmentation strategy: Always learning useful things*
Lawrence Phillips and Lisa Pearl

11:40 *Learning the hyperparameters to learn morphology*
Stella Frank

12:00 *An explicit statistical model of learning lexical segmentation using multiple cues*
Çağrı Çöltekin and John Nerbonne

12:30 Lunch break

Saturday April 26, 2014 (continued)

Invited Talk 2

2:00 *Distributional Learning as a Theory of Language Acquisition*
Alexander Clark

Session 2: Lexical acquisition and language evolution

2:50 *A multimodal corpus for the evaluation of computational models for (grounded) language acquisition*
Judith Gaspers, Maximilian Panzner, Andre Lemme, Philipp Cimiano, Katharina J. Rohlfing and Sebastian Wrede

3:20 Coffee Break

3:45 *Towards a computational model of grammaticalization and lexical diversity*
Christian Bentz and Paula Buttery

4:05 *How well can a corpus-derived co-occurrence network simulate human associative behavior?*
Gemma Bel Enguix, Reinhard Rapp and Michael Zock

4:25 *Agent-based modeling of language evolution*
Torvald Lekvam, Björn Gambäck and Lars Bungum

Session 3: Second language acquisition

4:45 *Missing Generalizations: A Supervised Machine Learning Approach to L2 Written Production*
Daniel Wiechmann and Elma Kerz

5:15 Closing

Challenging incrementality in human language processing: two operations for a cognitive architecture

Philippe Blache
Aix-Marseille Université & CNRS
LPL (UMR7309), 13100, Aix-en-Provence, France
blache@blri.fr

The description of language complexity and the cognitive load related to the different linguistic phenomena is a key issue for the understanding of language processing. Many studies have focused on the identification of specific parameters that can lead to a simplification or on the contrary to a complexification of the processing (e.g. the different difficulty models proposed in (Gibson, 2000), (Warren and Gibson, 2002), (Hawkins, 2001)). Similarly, different simplification factors can be identified, such as the notion of activation, relying on syntactic priming effects making it possible to predict (or activate) a word (Vasishth, 2003). Several studies have shown that complexity factors are cumulative (Keller, 2005), but can be offset by simplification (Blache et al., 2006). It is therefore necessary to adopt a global point of view of language processing, explaining the interplay between positive and negative cumulativity, in other words compensation effects.

From the computational point of view, some models can account more or less explicitly for these phenomena. This is the case of the Surprisal index (Hale, 2001), offering for each word an assessment of its integration costs into the syntactic structure. This evaluation is done starting from the probability of the possible solutions. On their side, symbolic approaches also provide an estimation of the activation degree, depending on the number and weight of syntactic relations to the current word (Blache et al., 2006); (Blache, 2013).

These approaches are based on the classical idea that language processing is incremental and occurs word by word. There are however several experimental evidences showing that a higher level of processing is used by human subjects. Eye-tracking data show for example that fixations are done by chunks, not by words (Rauzy and Blache, 2012). Similarly, EEG experiments have shown that processing multiword expressions (for example idioms) relies on global mechanisms (Vespignani et al., 2010); (Rommers et al., 2013).

Starting from the question of complexity and its estimation, I will address in this presentation the problem of language processing and its organization. I propose more precisely, using computational complexity models, to define a cohesion index between words. Such an index makes it possible to define chunks (or more generally units) that are built directly, by aggregation, instead of syntactic analysis. In this hypothesis, parsing consists in two different processes: aggregation and integration.

Acknowledgments

This work, carried out within the Labex BLRI (ANR-11-LABX-0036), has benefited from support from the French government, managed by the French National Agency for Research (ANR), under the project title Investments of the Future A*MIDEX (ANR-11-IDEX-0001-02).

Short biography

Philipe Blache is Senior Researcher at CNRS (Aix-Marseille University, France). He is the Director of the BLRI (*Brain and Language Research Institute*), federating 6 research laboratories in Linguistics, Computer Science, Psychology and Neurosciences.

Philippe Blache earned an MA in Linguistics from Université de Provence and a MSc in Computer Science from Université de la Méditerranée, where he received in 1990 his PhD in Artificial Intelligence.

During his career, Philippe Blache has focused on Natural Language Processing and Formal Linguistics, with a special interest in spoken language analysis. He has proposed a linguistic theory, called *Property Grammars*, suitable for describing language in its different uses, and explaining linguistic domains interaction. His current academic works address the question of human language processing and its complexity.

Philippe Blache has been director of two CNRS laboratories in France (2LC and LPL). He has served on numerous boards (European Chapter of the ACL, ESSLLI standing committee, CSLP, etc.). He is currently member of the Scientific Council of Aix-Marseille Université, member of the "Comité National de la Recherche Scientifique" in computer science and he chairs the TALN conference standing committee.

References

Philippe Blache, Barbara Hemforth, and Stéphane Rauzy. 2006. Acceptability prediction by means of grammaticality quantification. In *ACL-44: Proceedings of the 21st International Conference on Computational Linguistics and the 44th annual meeting of the Association for Computational Linguistics*. Association for Computational Linguistics, July.

Philippe Blache. 2013. Chunks et activation : un modèle de facilitation du traitement linguistique. In *Proceedings of TALN-2014*.

Edward Gibson. 2000. The Dependency Locality Theory: A Distance-Based Theory of Linguistic Complexity. In Alec Marantz, Yasushi Miyashita, and Wayne O'Neil, editors, *Image, Language, Brain*, pages 95–126. Cambridge, Massachussetts, MIT Press.

John Hale. 2001. A probabilistic earley parser as a psycholinguistic model. In *Proceeding of 2nd Conference of the North American Chapter of the Association for Computational Linguistics*, Pittsburgh, PA.

John Hawkins. 2001. Why are categories adjacent. *Journal of Linguistics*, 37.

Frank Keller. 2005. Linear Optimality Theory as a Model of Gradience in Grammar. In *Gradience in Grammar: Generative Perspectives*. Oxford University Press.

Stéphane Rauzy and Philippe Blache. 2012. Robustness and processing difficulty models. a pilot study for eye-tracking data on the french treebank. In *Proceedings of the 1st Eye-Tracking and NLP workshop*.

Joost Rommers, Antje S Meyer, Peter Praamstra, and Falk Huettig. 2013. Neuropsychologia. *Neuropsychologia*, 51(3):437–447, February.

Shravan Vasishth. 2003. Quantifying processing difficulty in human sentence parsing: The role of decay, activation, and similarity-based interference. In *Proceedings of the European Cognitive Science Conference 2003*.

Francesco Vespignani, Paolo Canal, Nicola Molinaro, Sergio Fonda, and Cristina Cacciari. 2010. Predictive mechanisms in idiom comprehension. *Journal of Cognitive Neuroscience*, 22(8):1682–1700.

Tessa Warren and Ted Gibson. 2002. The influence of referential processing on sentence complexity. *Cognition*, 85:79–112.

A Brazilian Portuguese Phonological-prosodic Algorithm Applied to Language Acquisition: A Case Study

Vera Vasilévski
Federal University of Santa Catarina (UFSC-CAPES)
Florianópolis, Brazil
sereiad@hotmail.com

Helena Ferro Blasi
Federal University of Santa Catarina (UFSC)
Florianópolis, Brazil
helena.blasi@ufsc.br

Márcio José Araújo
Federal University of Technology of Paraná (UTFPR)
Curitiba, Brazil
marciomjapr@gmail.com

Abstract

The paper presents a system for transcribing and annotating phonological information in Brazilian Portuguese, including syllabification. An application of this system for the assessment of language understanding and production is described, following a child longitudinally, comparing expected production with observed production.

1 Introduction

We present an application of a phonological-prosodic algorithm which converts Brazilian Portuguese graphemes to phonological symbols. For a better understanding, a brief report about the origin of the algorithm, altogether with some theoretical comments are presented, before the case study of the phonological processes found in the speech samples of a child. Sessions were recorded, until the complete acquisition of all Portuguese phonemes by the child, which occurred in the fifth session.

In 2008, we created the first version of a phonological-prosodic algorithm for Brazilian Portuguese. Actually, it is the functional algorithm of the grapheme to phoneme converter Nhenhém (Vasilévski, 2008, 2012a, 2012b). It has all written Portuguese spelling rules, and also the entire Portuguese prosodic system. When that algorithm was built, we kept in mind its usefulness to different fields deeply related to phonology, such as speech therapy, allowing the study of children phonological disorders, and language acquisition.

We focus here on its application to language acquisition, allowing the study of children phonological acquisition processes. Hence, our objective is to show the phonological-prosodic algorithm usefulness to language survey, from a practical point of view, by showing the process involved in the last stages of the acquisition of Portuguese phonology.

For a better understanding of the application and of the case study, the paper starts with some theory on phonological acquisition, then, some aspects of Brazilian Portuguese acquisition are presented.

2 Phonological Development

Studies of first language acquisition tend to support the view that the ability for language is innate in healthy human beings, and that its appearance can be predicted as part of the normal development of any child, given the right environment (Beaken, 1971).

The greatest expansion of the phonological system is observed from 1 year and six months old up to 4 years old, when there is an increase of the phonetic inventory of most complex syllable structures and, therefore, a period characterized by the occurrence of omissions, substitutions, as well as other phonological processes (Wertzner, 2004).

A phonological process is a mental operation that applies in speech to substitute, for a class of sounds or sound sequences presenting a specific common difficulty to the speech capacity of the individual, an alternative class identical but lacking the difficult property (Stampe, 1973).

It is worth remembering that, at the richest stage of normal language development (1 year and a half to 4 years old, as said), inappropriate sound gestures are expected phonological processes that relate to children's adaptations, until they automate the adult speech patterns. Thus, the phonological processes – that are natural and inborn – guide the facilitation of complex vocal gestures and their planning, until children reach the adult performance.

Moreover, the early-acquired competence is filtered through an increasing number of phonological transformations to produce, finally, a mature performance. Although the mature phonemic system is acquired at an early stage, articulation may not be completely mature until after 7 years. Even though most children can be said to have mastered the complete set of potential phonemic oppositions of adult language by the age of 4 years – in other words, their phonological competence is established – yet, in adult terms, their performance falls short of their competence, in that they are unable to produce many of the gestures of mature articulation of the phonemes. Development after this stage takes place in the maturing of articulation, and in the acquisition of the complex transformations which operate on the basic acquired competence, to produce forms of speech similar to those heard from mature speakers (Beaken, 1971).

2.1 Some Aspects of Brazilian Portuguese Phonological Acquisition

Regarding phonemes, Brazilian Portuguese has 21 consonants (/p/, /b/, /f/, /v/, /m/, /n/, /t/, /d/, /s/, /z/, /l/, /ʎ/, /r/, /ʀ/, /ʃ/, /ʒ/, /ɲ/, /k/, /g/, and the archiphonemes |R|, |S|), and 14 vowels (/a/, /e/, /ɛ/, /i/, /o/, /ɔ/, /u/, /j/, /w/, /ã/, /ẽ/, /ĩ/, /õ/, /ũ/) (Scliar-Cabral, 2003a; Câmara Jr., 1986, 1977; Vasilévski, 2012a).

Lateral liquid phonemes /l/ and /ʎ/ and non-lateral liquid /r/ and /ʀ/ are the latest to be acquired in Brazilian Portuguese. Furthermore, such acquisition is marked by intense use of diversified phonological processes. What perhaps justifies this late acquisition, in Brazilian Portuguese as well as in other systems, is that this class is very complex, both in articulation and phonological aspects (Lamprecht, 2004).

Within this group of sounds, lateral phonemes are acquired before the non-lateral ones. The first lateral phoneme to be stabilized by children is /l/, which is subdued before the emergence of the first non-lateral liquid phoneme /ʀ/. This occurs with the phonemes /ʎ/ – graphically lh – and /r/, being the first acquired before the second (Hernandorena and Lamprecht, 1997). In Portuguese, the phoneme /r/ occurs: 1) forming a syllable with an oral or nasal vowel (simple onset); 2) in second position of inseparable consonant clusters, preceding oral or nasal vowel (complex onset); and 3) in syllable ending (coda, when it is the archiphoneme |R|). See Tab.1 for examples.

In most cases, the acquisition of the phoneme /r/ happens initially in the position of simple onset (by 4 years old) and then in the position of complex onset (by 5 years old), the acquisition of the phoneme /r/ in coda position (that is, |R|) occurs by 4 years old (Lamprecht, 2004) either.

Another linguistic phenomenon to be taken into account is diphthongization. It happens when one vowel breaks into two segments, where the first one matches the original vowel and the second (/j/ or /w/) is harmonic with the nature of the triggering vowel. In Brazilian Portuguese, one of the conditions when diphthongization occurs, and that matters here, is thus defined: a stressed vowel, followed by a devoiced alveolar fricative [s], in the ending syllable of a word, becomes diphthongized by the addition of a second segment, an [i] (Cagliari, 2002). Since diphthongization is a strengthening process, it occurs preferentially with strong vowels, and, in Romance languages, /a/ is the strongest vowel, and /i/, the weakest (Foley, 1977). The semivowels of stressed syllables can be either produced or not in speech, both options belonging to Portuguese language system (Vasilévski, 2012a). From the linguistic point of view, diphthongization is strongly related to the geographical dialectal variation (Leiria, 2000).

3 A Program for Helping Language Acquisition Research

By using Nhenhém phonological-prosodic algorithm, we built Nhenhém Fonoaud – NhFonoaud –, an application for assisting speech therapy, and so language acquisition. We began covering just one phonological process, called “unvoicedness”: a substitution of a voiced sound for an unvoiced one (e.g. /b/ → /p/) (Blasi and Vasilévski, 2011). Soon, we realized that the phonological-prosodic algorithm could cover much more.

One of the motivations for creating such a system is that many Brazilian language acquisition researchers record their collected data using orthographic representation. As a result, those transcriptions are idiosyncratic and cannot be properly generalized, since they lack patterns. Data must be recorded in a phonologic-phonetic format, essential for these studies, since they address phonological processes.

According to researchers and speech therapists, there is no similar work in Brazilian Portuguese. Probably, there are similar initiatives for other languages, and we expect to make comparisons soon.

3.1 The decoder Nhenhém Phonological-prosodic Algorithm

Nhenhém (/ɲẽ.ˈɲẽj/) is a computational program that decodes Brazilian's official writing system into phonological symbols and marks prosody (Vasilévski, 2008, 2012a). In 2010, we augmented its main algorithm, so the system became able of providing the phonological syllabic division and the spelling syllabic division, with at least 99% of accuracy (see Vasilévski, 2012a, 2012b for more details). Then we developed an automatic syllable parsing (Vasilévski, 2010).

In 2012, we made some adjustments regarding morphology, and solved the unpredictable situations brought, for example, by the prefix "trans-" that can be either decoded as /trãz/ or /trãs/, in consequence of resyllabification (see Vasilévski, 2012a). NhFonoaud benefits of all improvements obtained by the basic algorithm.

3.2 Nhenhém Fonoaud

The application of Nhenhém phonological-prosodic algorithm to language acquisition and speech therapy has been presented (Blasi and Vasilévski, 2011, Vasilévski, 2012a, 2012b), but this is the first time that a case study is discussed.

The first major challenge of working with phonemic transcription is the consistency of data. Different research questions require different levels of representation (Albert et al., 2013). In this regard, relying on an orthographic representation of speech, when dealing with language acquisition, does not make sense.

The program supports the analysis of processes that occur in the child's phonological system, through the automatic phonological transcription simultaneously to samples of the child speech recording. Thus, data relies on a phonemic representation of speech, automatically done by the algorithm, through Nhenhém Fonoaud.

NhFonoaud is designed for dealing with phonological tests, using words wittingly grouped to analyze specific aspects of speech and phenomena involved in its development. One of the tools of the program was the tests battery called Reception and Production of Spoken Language Assessment (Scliar-Cabral, 2003b). These tests were elaborated for assessing overt symptoms of spoken language reception and production problems. The first step is assessing phonetic features perception, namely, the ability of distinguishing minimal pairs, what means distinguishing Brazilian Portuguese words.

The battery is composed by 81 pictures that represent specific words in Portuguese. The pictures are grouped into cards of six elements each. There are 15 cards, and some pictures appear in more than one. Each card is assembled to address the perception and production of one specific phonetic feature: 1) /v/-/f/, /p/-/b/, /t/-/d/; 2) /k/-/g/, /ʃ/-/ʒ/, /s/-/z/; 3) /m/-/n/, /t/-/d/, /s/-/f/; 4) /b/-/g/, /f/-/r/, /k/-/p/; 5) /t/-/k/, |R|-/s/, /l/-/ʎ/; 6) /t/-/s/, /k/-|R|, /p/-/f/; 7) /d/-/t/, /t/-/r/, /d/-/s/; 8) /m/-/b/, /n/-/r/, /z/-/n/; 9) /ɲ/-/ʎ/, /d/-/n/, /n/-/l/; 10) /r/-/l/ (in three different contexts); 11) /ɛ/-/ɔ/, /i/-/u/, /e/-/o/; 12) /i/-/e/, /ĩ/-/ẽ/, /u/-/o/; 13) /e(j)/-/ɛ/, /o/-/ɔ/, /ɔ/-/o(w)/; 14) /ɔ/-/a/, /m/-/b/ (in two different contexts)/; 15) /ẽ/-/e/, /o/-/õ/, /a/-/ã/.

In the reception battery, the speech therapist, behind the child, says the word and the child must point to one of the six pictures in each card. In the production battery, the speech therapist points to one of the six pictures in each card and the child must label it.

While the child labels the picture, the researcher can edit the canonical transcription provided by the program to match the child's production. For example, writing the lateral phoneme, when the child produces it, instead of the vibrating one.

In principle, four situations may happen during the assessment (Fig.1): the child does not recognize the picture (NR); the child gives the

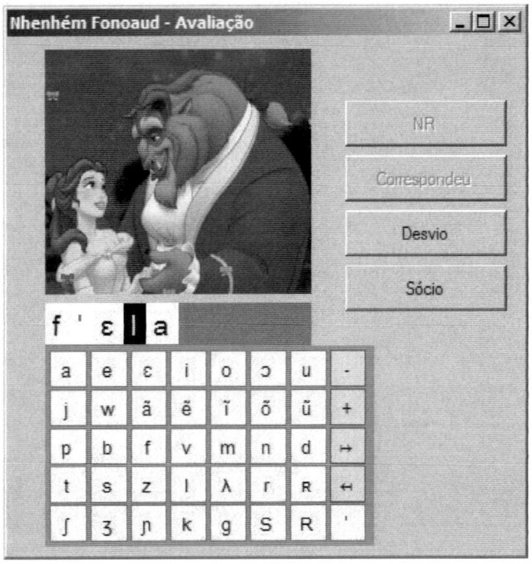

Figure 1. A register screen of Nhenhém Fonoaud
Picture: Beauty and the Beast. Disney©.

expected response (Correspondeu); the child gives an unexpected response (deviation – Desvio); the child translates the word into his/her sociolinguistic variety (not deviation – Sócio).

NhFonoaud stores the records and compares them with the transcription expected, for generating reports. Hence, it is possible to build a corpus, to retrieve it, grouping it according to date, situation, child's age, type of card (test); then it is possible the conversion into numbers, using different formats, comparing the phonological transcription and the correspondent audio, and the recorded sessions. Therefore, it facilitates child's progress monitoring.

In spite of working with words, NhFonoaud can be adjusted to work with bigger texts, formed by many sentences. For the purpose of assessing the child phonemic system, using minimal pairs and small sentences is enough.

3.3 Testing Nhenhém Fonoaud

The data analysis that we now present refers to a child in a clear process of language acquisition. It is based on oral emissions of a girl that we will call Inês. The 15 cards (Scliar-Cabral, 2003b) were applied, covering all the Brazilian Portuguese phonemes. Five sessions were recorded, starting when Inês was 2 years, 11 months, and 8 days; until she was 3 years, 8 months and 29 days.

Inês was born in Curitiba, Brazil, of Brazilian parents. She was not considered to have significant hearing loss. The child had developed some computer skills. Data was collected by her parents, by showing her the cards at the computer, during a daily conversation. Inês had already contact with the pictures, and had learned some names that were not part of her daily life. The sessions were recorded by using the audio resources of the same computer, and the records were clear enough to be used in this study.

3.3.1 Testing results

The results reveal the phonological processes used by Inês. Four were observed in her emissions: two of substitution, one of deletion, and one of adding. From the reports generated by Nhenhém Fonoaud, we created Tab 1.

So, at the age of 2y11m8d, three phonological processes relate to a single phoneme of her mother tongue, the non-lateral, vibrating /r/, and another one to diphthongization. Thus, Inês is only unable to produce the most complex Portuguese phoneme, in anyone of the three cases in which it occurs. The first session reveals that the child is able to produce all the vowels (14) of her mother tongue and 20 consonantal phonemes among the 21 of Brazilian Portuguese. No changes are observed for about 4 months, but this is expected, since progress in language is

Spelling	***Meaning***	***Expected sounds***	***Emitted sounds***				
			2y11m8d	3y2m23d	3y6m25d	3y7m24d	3y8m29d
porta	door	/pˈɔRta/	[pˈɔjta]	[pˈɔjta]	[pˈɔjta]	[pˈɔrta]	[pˈɔrta]
torta	pie	/tˈɔRta/	[tˈɔjta]	[tˈɔjta]	[tˈɔjta]	[tˈɔjta]	[tˈɔrta]
porco	pig	/pˈoRku/	[pˈojku]	[pˈojku]	[pˈojku]	[pˈorku]	[pˈorku]
		Process:	A	A	A	A	-
barata	cockroach	/barˈata/	[balˈata]	[balˈata]	[balˈata]	[barˈata]	[barˈata]
pera	pear	/pˈera/	[pˈela]	[pˈela]	[pˈela]	[pˈera]	[pˈera]
mureta	a low wall	/murˈeta/	[mulˈeta]	[mulˈeta]	[murˈeta]	[murˈeta]	[murˈeta]
perada	pear jelly	/perˈada/	[pelˈada]	[pelˈada]	[perˈada]	[perˈada]	[perˈada]
vara	fish rod	/vˈara/	[vˈala]	[vˈala]	[vˈala]	[vˈara]	[vˈara]
feira	street market	/fˈera/	[fˈela]	[fˈela]	[fˈera]	[fˈera]	[fˈera]
fera	beast	/fˈɛra/	[fˈɛla]	[fˈɛla]	[fˈɛra]	[fˈɛra]	[fˈɛra]
		Process:	B	B	B	-	-
traça	bookworm	/trˈasa/	[tˈasa]	[tˈasa]	[tˈlasa]	[tˈrasa]	[tˈrasa]
trança	braid	/trˈãsa/	[tˈãsa]	[tˈãsa]	[tˈlãsa]	[tˈrãsa]	[tˈrãsa]
trens	trains	/trẽjS/	[tẽjs]	[tẽjs]	[tlẽjs]	[tlẽjs]	[trẽjs]
três	three	/treS/	[tejs]	[tejs]	[tlejs]	[trejs]	[trejs]
		Process:	C/D	C/D	B/D	B/D	D

Phonological processes	
A	Substitution of the non-lateral, vibrating sound |R| or /r/ for the glide sound /j/ (semivowelization)
B	Substitution of the non-lateral, vibrating sound /r/ for the lateral liquid sound /l/
C	Reduction of the consonant cluster plosive+non-lateral /tr/ to the single sound /t/
D	Diphthongization through insertion of a vowel in the last syllable of words ending with vowel+|S|.

Table 1. Phonological processes used by Inês.

never regular; it may proceed at a fast rate for some periods while at others very little seems to be happening (Beaken, 1971). Then, the sound /r/ is emerging, only in simple onset, and she produces the cluster, but says /tl/ instead of /tr/ (3y6m25d). One month later (3y7m24d), she starts producing /r/ in coda position and the cluster /tr/, with some difficult yet. The sound /r/ in simple onset is naturally produced. One more month (3y8m29d), and she is able to naturally produce /r/ in all the contexts it happens in Portuguese, and keeps diphthongization.

Regarding diphthongization, it happens when the child inserts the semivowel /j/ between a vowel and the coda |S|, creating a diphthong. This circumstance advises that the child is adjusting her speech according to adult speech, since the region where Inês lives is where this phonological phenomenon occurs most, considering the South of Brazil (Leiria, 2000). It is a trait of the child's sociolinguistic variety, dependent upon geographic factor, and so she keeps saying it.

Hence, this research found that Inês completed the acquisition of the phonemes of her native language at 3 years and 8 months approximately, in normal development.

4 Conclusion and Outlooks

We briefly presented a system for dealing with phonological information in Brazilian Portuguese, and a case study from it, that is, the longitudinal speech recording of a child – the girl called Inês. Data allowed to know the last processes involved in the acquisition of the phonemes of her mother tongue.

From the preliminary results obtained, it is possible to conclude that Nhenhém Fonoaud can be helpful to language acquisition research. Nevertheless, the usefulness of the phonological prosodic algorithm has to be proven, by testing it in different situations, such as deviant language acquisition, speech therapy, and also other researches. This will be our next step.

Reference

Aviad Albert, Brian MacWhinney, Bracha Nir, Shuly Wintner. 2013. The Hebrew CHILDES Corpus Transcription and Morphological Analysis. *Language resources and evaluation*. Springer, Netherlands.

Beauty and the Beast. 2013. Disney© downloads. Available from http://disney.go.com/disneyvideos/animatedfilms/beauty/downloads.html

Carmen Lúcia M. Hernandorena and Regina R. Lamprecht. 1997. A aquisição das consoantes líquidas do português. *Letras de Hoje*, Porto Alegre, 32(4):7-22.

David Stampe. *A dissertation on natural phonology*. 1973. PhD Thesis, University of Chicago.

Haydée F. Wertzner. 2004. Fonologia: Desenvolvimento e Alterações. In: LP Ferreira, DM Befi-Lopes and SCO Limongi. *Tratado de Fonoaudiologia*. Roca, São Paulo, 772-786.

James Foley. 1977. *Foundations of theoretical phonology*. Cambridge University Press, Cambridge.

Helena F. Blasi and Vera Vasilévski. 2011. Programa piloto para transcrição fonética automática na clínica fonoaudiológica. *Documentos para el XVI Congresso Internacional de la ALFAL*, Universidad de Alcalá, Alcalá de Henares/Madrid.

Joaquim M. Câmara Jr. 1986. *Estrutura da língua portuguesa*. 16.ed. Vozes, Petrópolis, RJ.

Joaquim M. Câmara Jr. 1977. *Para o estudo da fonêmica portuguesa*. 2.ed. Padrão, Rio de Janeiro.

Leonor Scliar-Cabral. 2003a. *Princípios do sistema alfabético do português do Brasil*. Contexto, São Paulo.

Leonor Scliar-Cabral. 2003b. *Guia prático de alfabetização*. Contexto, São Paulo.

Lúcia Lovato Leiria. 2000. A ditongação variável em sílabas tônicas finais travadas por /S/. *Organon*, 14(28/29):133-141.

Luiz Carlos Cagliari. 2002. *Análise fonológica: introdução à teoria e à prática*. Mercado das Letras, Campinas, São Paulo, Brazil.

Michael Alan Beaken. 1971. *A study of phonological development in a primary school population of East London*. PhD Thesis. London University. http://discovery.ucl.ac.uk/1317623/1/261970.pdf

Nhenhém®. 2008-2011. Grapheme do phoneme converter for Brazilian Portuguese. INPI 1265-1.

Regina R. Lamprecht. 2004. *Aquisição fonológica do Português: Perfil de desenvolvimento e subsídios para terapia*. Artmed, Porto Alegre.

Vera Vasilévski. 2012a. *Descodificación automática de la lengua escrita de Brasil basada en reglas fonológicas*. Saarbrücken, Editorial Académica Española, Germany.

Vera Vasilévski. 2012b. Phonologic Patterns of Brazilian Portuguese: a grapheme to phoneme converter based study. *Proceedings of the EACL, Workshop on Computational Models of Language Acquisition and Loss*. University of Avignon, France.

Vera Vasilévski. 2011. O hífen na separação silábica automática. *Revista do Simpósio de Estudos Lingüísticos e Literários – SELL*, 1(3):657-676.

Vasilévski, Vera. 2008. *Construção de um programa computacional para suporte à pesquisa em fonologia do português do Brasil*. PhD Thesis. Universidade Federal de Santa Catarina, Florianópolis, Brasil.

Bayesian inference as a cross-linguistic word segmentation strategy: Always learning useful things

Lawrence Phillips and Lisa Pearl
Department of Cognitive Sciences
University of California, Irvine
{lawphill, lpearl}@uci.edu

Abstract

Statistical learning has been proposed as one of the earliest strategies infants could use to segment words out of their native language because it does not rely on language-specific cues that must be derived from existing knowledge of the words in the language. Statistical word segmentation strategies using Bayesian inference have been shown to be quite successful for English (Goldwater et al. 2009), even when cognitively inspired processing constraints are integrated into the inference process (Pearl et al. 2011, Phillips & Pearl 2012). Here we test this kind of strategy on child-directed speech from seven languages to evaluate its effectiveness cross-linguistically, with the idea that a viable strategy should succeed in each case. We demonstrate that Bayesian inference is indeed a viable cross-linguistic strategy, provided the goal is to identify useful units of the language, which can range from sub-word morphology to whole words to meaningful word combinations.

1 Introduction

Word segmentation is one of the first tasks children must complete when learning their native language, and infants are able to identify words in fluent speech by around 7.5 months (Jusczyk & Aslin 1995; Echols et al. 1997; Jusczyk et al., 1993)). Proposals for learning strategies that can accomplish this (Saffran et al. 1996) have centered on language-independent cues that are not derived from existing knowledge of words. Bayesian inference is a statistical strategy operating over transitional probability that has been shown to be successful for identifying words in English, whether the salient perceptual units are phonemes (Goldwater et al. 2009 [**GGJ**], Pearl et al. 2011 [**PGS**]) or syllables (Phillips & Pearl 2012 [**P&P**]), and whether the inference process is optimal (GGJ, PGS) or constrained by cognitive limitations that children may share (PGS, P&P). It may, however, be the case that these strategies work well for English, but not other languages (Fourtassi et al. 2013). Therefore, we evaluate this same learning strategy on seven languages with different linguistic profiles: English, German, Spanish, Italian, Farsi, Hungarian, and Japanese. If Bayesian inference is a viable strategy for word segmentation, it should succeed on all languages. While some attempts have been made to evaluate Bayesian word segmentation strategies on languages other than English (e.g., Sesotho: Johnson 2008, Blanchard et al. 2010), this is the first evaluation on a significant range of languages that we are aware of.

We assume the relevant perceptual units are syllables, following previous modeling work (Swingly 2005, Gambell & Yang 2006, Lignos & Yang 2010, Phillips & Pearl 2012) that draws from experimental evidence that infants younger than 7.5 months are able to perceive syllables but not phonemes (Werker & Tees 1984, Juszyck & Derrah 1987, Eimas 1999). We demonstrate that Bayesian word segmentation is a successful cross-linguistic learning strategy, provided we define success in a more practical way than previous word segmentation studies have done. We consider a segmentation strategy successful if it identifies units useful for subsequent language acquisition processes (e.g., meaning learning, structure learning). Thus, not only is the orthographic gold standard typically used in word segmentation tasks acceptable, but also productive morphology and coherent chunks made up of multiple words. This serves as a general methodological contribution about the definition of segmentation success, especially when considering that the meaningful units across the world's languages may vary.

2 The Bayesian learning strategy

Bayesian models are well suited to questions of language acquisition because they distinguish between the learner's pre-existing beliefs (prior) and how the learner evaluates incoming data (likelihood), using Bayes' theorem:

$$P(h|d) \propto P(d|h)P(h)$$

The Bayesian learners we evaluate are the optimal learners of GGJ and the constrained learners of PGS. All learners are based on the same underlying models from GGJ. The first of these models assumes independence between words (a *unigram* assumption) while the second assumes that a word depends on the word before it (a *bigram* assumption). To encode these assumptions into the model, GGJ use a Dirichlet Process (Ferguson, 1973), which supposes that the observed sequence of words $w_1 \ldots w_n$ is generated sequentially using a probabilistic generative process. In the unigram case, the identity of the *i*th word is chosen according to:

$$P(w_i = w|w_1 \ldots w_{i-1}) = \frac{n_{i-1}(w)+\alpha P_0(w)}{i-1+\alpha} \quad (1)$$

where $n_{i-1}(w)$ is the number of times w appears in the previous $i - 1$ words, α is a free parameter of the model, and P_0 is a base distribution specifying the probability that a novel word will consist of the perceptual units $x_1 \ldots x_m$:

$$P(w = x_1 \ldots x_m) = \prod_{j=1}^{m} P(x_j) \quad (2)$$

In the bigram case, a hierarchical Dirichlet Process (Teh et al. 2006) is used. This model additionally tracks the frequencies of two-word sequences and is defined as:

$$P(w_i = w|w_{i-1} = w', w_1 \ldots w_{i-2}) = \frac{n_{i-1}(w',w)+\beta P_1(w)}{n_{i-1}(w')+\beta} \quad (3)$$

$$P_1(w_i = w) = \frac{b_{i-1}(w)+\gamma P_0(w)}{b_{i-1}+\gamma} \quad (4)$$

where $n_{i-1}(w',w)$ is the number of times the bigram (w',w) has occurred in the first $i - 1$ words, $b_{i-1}(w)$ is the number of times w has occurred as the second word of a bigram, b_{i-1} is the total number of bigrams, and β and γ are free model parameters.[1]

In both the unigram and bigram case, the model implicitly incorporates preferences for smaller lexicons by preferring words that appear frequently (due to (1) and (3)) and preferring shorter words in the lexicon (due to (2) and (4)).

The **BatchOpt** learner for this model is taken from GGJ and uses Gibbs sampling (Geman & Geman 1984) to run over the entire input in a single batch, sampling every potential word boundary 20,000 times. We consider this learner "optimal" in that it is unconstrained by cognitive considerations. We also evaluate the constrained learners developed by PGS that incorporate processing and memory constraints into the learning process.

The **OnlineOpt** learner incorporates a basic processing limitation: linguistic processing occurs online rather than in batch after a period of data collection. Thus, the OnlineOpt learner processes one utterance at a time, rather than processing the entire input at once. This learner uses the Viterbi algorithm to converge on the local optimal word segmentation for the current utterance, conditioned on all utterances seen so far.

The **OnlineSubOpt** learner is similar to the OnlineOpt learner in processing utterances incrementally, but is motivated by the idea that infants are not optimal decision-makers. Infants may not *always* select the best segmentation, and instead sample segmentations based on their perceived probabilities. The OnlineSubOpt learners will often choose the best segmentation but will occasionally choose less likely alternatives, based on the probability associated with each segmentation. The Forward algorithm is used to compute the likelihood of all possible segmentations and then a segmentation is chosen based on the resulting distribution.

The **OnlineMem** learner also processes data incrementally, but uses a Decayed Markov Chain Monte Carlo algorithm (Marthi et al. 2002) to implement a kind of limited short-term memory. This learner is similar to the original GGJ ideal (BatchOpt) learner in that it uses something like Gibbs sampling. However, the OnlineMem learner does not sample all potential boundaries; instead, it samples some number s of previous boundaries using the decay function b^{-d} to select the boundary to sample; b is the number of potential boundary locations between the boundary under consideration b_c and the end of

---

[1] Parameters for the unigram and bigram models underlying all learners were chosen to maximize the performance of the BatchOpt learner, discussed below. English: α=1, β=1, γ=90; German: α=1, β=1, γ=100; Spanish: α=1, β=200, γ=50; Italian: α=1, β=20, γ=200; Farsi: α=1, β=200, γ=500; Hungarian: α=1, β=300, γ=500; Japanese: α=1, β=300, γ=100

the current utterance while d is the decay rate. Thus, the further b_c is from the end of the current utterance, the less likely it is to be sampled. Larger values of d indicate a stricter memory constraint. All our results here use a set, non-optimized value for d of 1.5, which was chosen to implement a heavy memory constraint (e.g., 90% of samples come from the current utterance, while 96% are in the current or previous utterances). Having sampled a set of boundaries[2], the learner can then update its beliefs about those boundaries and subsequently update its lexicon.

3 Cross-linguistic input

We evaluate the Bayesian learner on input derived from child-directed speech corpora in seven languages: English, German, Spanish, Italian, Farsi, Hungarian and Japanese. All corpora were taken from the CHILDES database (MacWhinney, 2000). When corpora were available only in orthographic form, they were first converted into the appropriate phonemic form. Afterwards, the corpora were syllabified. Where possible, we utilized adult syllabification judgments. All other words were syllabified using the Maximum-Onset principle, which states that the beginning of a syllable should be as large as possible, without violating the language's phonotactic constraints.

Our corpora vary in a number of important ways. Although we attempt to limit our corpora to early child-directed speech, some of our corpora contain speech directed to children as old as age five (e.g. Farsi). Many of our corpora do, however, consist entirely of early child-directed speech (e.g., English, Japanese). Similarly, the same amount of data is not always easily available for each language. Our shortest corpus (German) consists of 9,378 utterances, while the longest (Farsi) consists of 31,657.

The languages themselves also contain many differences that potentially affect syllable-based word segmentation. While our English and Hungarian corpora contain 2,330 and 3,029 unique syllables, respectively, Japanese and Spanish contain only 526 and 524, respectively. Some languages may be easier to segment than others based on distributional factors. Fourtassi et al. (2013) show, for example, that English has less ambiguous segmentation than Japanese. In addition, the languages also have differences in their syntax and morphology. For example, Hungarian and Japanese are both agglutinative languages that have more regular morphological systems, while English, German, Spanish, Italian and Farsi are all fusional languages to varying degrees. If a language has regular morphology, an infant might reasonably segment out morphemes rather than words. This highlights the need for a more flexible metric of segmentation performance: A segmentation strategy which identifies units useful for later linguistic analysis should not be penalized.

4 Learning results & discussion

We analyze our results in terms of word token F-scores, which is the harmonic mean of token precision and recall, where precision is the probability that a word segmented by the model is a true word (# identified true / # identified) and recall measures the probability that any true word was correctly identified (# identified true / total # true). F-scores range from 0 to 100, with higher values indicating better performance. Performance on all languages is presented in Table 1. An error analysis was conducted where we systematically counted the following "reasonable errors" as successful segmentation:

(i) Mis-segmentations resulting in real words. For example, the word "alright" might be oversegmented as "all right", resulting in two actual English words. Most languages show errors of this type, with more occurring for the bigram model, with the least in English (BatchOpt: 4.52%) and most in Spanish (BatchOpt: 23.97%). We restrict these errors to words which occur minimally ten times in the corpus in order to avoid accepting errors in the corpora or nonsense syllables as real words.

(ii) Productive morphology. Given the syllabic nature of our corpora, only syllabic morphology can be identified. Languages like English, Spanish and Italian have relatively few errors that produce morphemes (e.g., BatchOpt: 0.13%, 0.05%, and 1.13% respectively), while Japanese, with more syllabic morphology has many such errors (e.g., BatchOpt: 4.69%).

[2] All OnlineMem learners sample s=20,000 boundaries per utterance. For a syllable-based learner, this works out to approximately 74% less processing than the BatchOpt learner (P&P).

		English	German	Spanish	Italian	Farsi	Hungarian	Japanese
Unigram	BatchOpt	55.70	73.43	64.28	70.48	72.48	64.01	69.11
	OnlineOpt	60.71	58.41	74.98	65.05	75.66	56.77	71.56
	OnlineSubOpt	65.76	70.95	77.15	66.48	74.89	60.21	71.73
	OnlineMem	58.68	73.85	67.78	66.77	67.31	60.07	70.49
Bigram	BatchOpt	80.19	84.15	80.34	79.36	76.01	70.87	73.11
	OnlineOpt	78.09	82.08	82.71	75.78	79.23	69.67	73.36
	OnlineSubOpt	80.44	82.03	80.75	73.59	67.54	65.48	66.14
	OnlineMem	89.58	88.83	83.27	74.08	73.98	69.48	73.24

Table 1. Token F-scores (presented as percents, from 0 to 100) for each learner across every language. Higher Token F-scores indicate better performance.

(iii) Common sequences of function words. For example, a learner might identify "is that a" as a single word, "isthata". These errors tend to be more common for unigram learners than bigram learners, which makes sense from a statistical standpoint since the unigram learner is unable to account for commonly occurring sequences of words and must do so by positing the collocation as a single word. Still, function word sequence errors are relatively uncommon in every language except German (e.g., BatchOpt: 21.73%)

Table 2 presents common examples of each type of acceptable error in English.

	True Word(s)	Model Output
Real words	something	some thing
	alright	all right
Morphology	going	go ing
	really	rea lly
Function word	you can	youcan
	are you	areyou

Table 2. Example reasonable errors of each type from English that result in real words, morphology, or function word collocations.

Generally speaking, the bigram learners tend to outperform the unigram learners, suggesting that the knowledge that words depend on previous words continues to be a useful one (as GGJ, PGS, and P&P found for English), though this difference may be small for some languages (e.g., Farsi, Japanese). Overall, performance for English and German is very high (best score: ~90%), while for other languages the learners tend to fare less well (best score: 70-83%), though still quite good. These results match previous work which indicated that English is particularly easy to segment compared to other languages (Johnson 2008; Blanchard et al. 2010; Fourtassi et al. 2013)

Importantly, the goal of early word segmentation is not for the infant to entirely solve word segmentation, but to get the word segmentation process started. Given this goal, Bayesian word segmentation seems effective for all these languages. Moreover, because our learners are looking for useful units, which can be realized in different ways across languages, they can identify foundational aspects of a language that are both smaller and larger than orthographic words.

5 Conclusion

We have demonstrated that Bayesian word segmentation performs quite well as an initial learning strategy for many different languages, so long as the learner is measured by how useful the units are that it identifies. This not only supports Bayesian word segmentation as a viable cross-linguistic strategy, but also suggests that a useful methodological norm for word segmentation research should be how well it identifies units that can scaffold future language acquisition. By taking into account reasonable errors that identify such units, we bring our model evaluation into alignment with the actual goal of early word segmentation.

References

Blanchard, D., Heinz, J., & Golinkoff, R. 2010. Modeling the contribution of phonotactic cues to the problem of word segmentation. *Journal of child language, 37*(3), 487.

Echols, C.H., Crowhurst, M.J. & Childers, J.B. 1997. The perception of rhythmic units in speech by infants and adults. *Journal of Memory and Language*, 36, 202-225.

Eimas, P.D. 1999. Segmental and syllabic representations in the perception of speech by young infants. *Journal of the Acoustical Society of America*, 105(3), 1901-1911.

Fourtassi, A., Börschinger, B., Johnson, M., & Dupoux, E. 2013. Whyisenglishsoeasytosegment? *Proceedings of the Fourth Annual Workshop on Cognitive Modeling and Computational Linguistics*, 1-10.

Gambell, T. & Yang, C. 2006. Word Segmentation: Quick but not dirty. Manuscript. New Haven: Yale University

Geman S. & Geman D. 1984. Stochastic Relaxation, Gibbs Distributions, and the Bayesian Restoration of Images. *IEEE Transactions on Pattern Analysis and Machine Intelligence,* 6, 721-741.

Goldwater, S., Griffiths, T. & Johnson, M. 2009. A Bayesian framework for word segmentation: Exploring the effects of context. *Cognition 112*(1), 21-54.

Johnson, M. 2008. Unsupervised word segmentation for Sesotho using adaptor grammars. *Proceedings of the Tenth Meeting of the ACL Special Interest Group on Computational Morphology and Phonology,* 20-27.

Jusczyk, P.W. & Derrah, C. 1987. Representation of speech sounds by young infants. *Developmental Psychology*, 23(5), 648-654.

Jusczyk, P.W., Cutler, A. & Redanz, N.J. 1993. Infants' preference for the predominant stress pattern of English words. *Child Development*, 64(3), 675-687.

Jusczyk, P.W. & Aslin, R.N. 1995. Infants' detection of the sound patterns of words in fluent speech. *Cognitive Psychology*, 29, 1-23.

Lignos, C. & Yang, C. 2010. Recession segmentation: Simpler online word segmentation using limited resources. *Proceedings of the Fourteenth Conference on Computational Natural Language Learning,* 88-97.

MacWhinney, B. 2000. *The CHILDES project: Tools for analyzing talk.* Mahwah, NJ: Lawrence Erlbaum Associates.

Marthi, B., Pasula, H., Russell, S. & Peres, Y., et al. 2002. Decayed MCMC filtering. In *Proceedings of 18th UAI,* 319-326.

Pearl, L., Goldwater, S., & Steyvers, M. 2011. Online Learning Mechanisms for Bayesian Models of Word Segmentation, *Research on Language and Computation*, special issue on computational models of language acquisition.

Phillips, L. & Pearl, L. 2012. "Less is more" in Bayesian word segmentation: When cognitively plausible learners outperform the ideal. In *Proceedings of the 34th Annual Conference of the Cognitive Science Society.*

Saffran, J.R., Aslin, R.N. & Newport, E.L. 1996. Statistical learning by 8-Month-Old Infants. *Science, 274*, 1926-1928.

Swingley, D. 2005. Statistical clustering and the contents of the infant vocabulary. *Cognitive Psychology, 50,* 86-132.

Teh, Y., Jordan, M., Beal, M., & Blei, D. 2006. Heirarchical Dirichlet processes. *Journal of the American Statistical Association, 101*(476), 1566-1581.

Werker, J.F. & Tees, R.C. 1984. Cross-language speech perception: Evidence for perceptual reorganization during the first year of life. *Infant Behavior & Development, 7,* 49-63.

Learning the hyperparameters to learn morphology

Stella Frank
ILCC, School of Informatics
University of Edinburgh
Edinburgh, EH8 9AB, UK
sfrank@inf.ed.ac.uk

Abstract

We perform hyperparameter inference within a model of morphology learning (Goldwater et al., 2011) and find that it affects model behaviour drastically. Changing the model structure successfully avoids the unsegmented solution, but results in oversegmentation instead.

1 Introduction

Bayesian models provide a sound statistical framework in which to explore aspects of language acquisition. Explicitly specifying the causal and computational structure of a model enables the investigation of hypotheses such as the feasibility of learning linguistic structure from the available input (Perfors et al., 2011), or the interaction of different linguistic levels (Johnson, 2008a). However, these models can be sensitive to small changes in (hyper-)parameters settings. Robustness in this respect is important, since positing specific parameter values is cognitively implausible.

In this paper we revisit a model of morphology learning presented by Goldwater and colleagues in Goldwater et al. (2006) and Goldwater et al. (2011) (henceforth GGJ). This model demonstrated the effectiveness of non-parametric stochastic processes, specifically the Pitman-Yor Process, for interpolating between types and tokens. Language learners are exposed to tokens, but many aspects of linguistic structure are lexical; identifying which tokens belong to the same lexical type is crucial. Surface form is not always sufficient, as in the case of ambiguous words. Moreover, morphology in particular is influenced by vocabulary-level type statistics (Bybee, 1995), so it is important for a model to operate on both levels: token statistics from realistic (child-directed) input, and type-level statistics based on the token analyses.

The GGJ model learns successfully given fixed hyperparameter values in the Pitman-Yor Process. However, we show that when these hyperparameters are inferred, it collapses to a token-based model with a trivial morphology. In this paper we discuss the reasons for this problematic behaviour, which are relevant for other models based on Pitman-Yor Processes with discrete base distributions, common in natural language tasks. We investigate some potential solutions, by changing the way morphemes are generated within the model. Our results are mixed; we avoid the hyperparameter problem, but learn overly compact morpheme lexicons.

2 The Pitman-Yor Process

The Pitman-Yor Process $G \sim \text{PYP}(a, b, H_0)$ (Pitman and Yor, 1997; Teh, 2006) generates distributions over the space of the base distribution H_0, with the hyperparameters a and b governing the extent of the shift from H_0. Draws from G have values from H_0, but with probabilities given by the PYP. For example, in a unigram PYP language model with observed words, H_0 may be a uniform distribution over the vocabulary, $U(\frac{1}{T})$. The PYP shifts this distribution to the power-law distribution over tokens found in natural language, allowing words to have much higher (and lower) than uniform probability. We will continue using the language model example in this section, since the subsequent morphology model is effectively a complex unigram language model in which word types correspond to morphological analyses. In our presentation, we pay particular attention to the role of the hyperparameter a, since this value governs the power-law behaviour of the PYP (Buntine and Hutter, 2010).

When G is marginalised out, the result is the PYP Chinese Restaurant Process, which is a useful representation of the distribution of observations (word tokens) to values from H_0 (types). In this restaurant, customers (tokens) arrive and are seated at one of a potentially infinite number of tables. Each table receives a dish (type) from the base distribution when the first customer is seated there; thereafter all subsequent customers adopt the same dish. The probability of customer z_i being seated at a table k depends on the number of customers already seated at that table n_k. Popular tables will attract more customers, generating a Zipfian distribution over customers at tables.

This Zipfian/power-law behaviour can be similar to that of the natural language data, and is the principal motivation behind using the PYP. However, it is only valid for the distribution of customers to tables. When the base distribution is discrete — as in our language model example and the morphology model — the same dish may be served at multiple tables. In most cases, the distribution of interest is generally that of customers (tokens) to dishes (types), rather than to tables, suggesting a preference for a setting in which each dish appears at few tables. This is dependent on a (constrained to be $0 \leq a < 1$), and to a lesser extent on b: If a is small, each dish will be served at a single table, resulting in the type-token and the table-customer power-laws matching. If a is near 1, however, the probability of more than a single customer being seated at a table is small, and the distribution of dishes being eaten by the customers will match the base distribution, rather than being adapted by the caching mechanism of the PYP.

The expected number of tables K grows as $O(N^a)$ (see Buntine and Hutter (2010) for an exact formulation). The number of word types in the data gives us a minimum number of tables, $K \geq T$. When a is small (less than 0.5), the number of expected tables is significantly less than the number of types in a non-trivial dataset, suggesting a lower bound for values of a.

In our language model, the posterior probability of assigning a word w_i to a table k with dish ℓ_k and n_k previous customers is:

$$p(w_i = k | w_1 \ldots w_{i-1}, a, b) \propto \tag{1}$$
$$\begin{cases} (n_k - a) I(w_i = \ell_k) & \text{if } 1 \leq k \leq K \\ (Ka + b) H_0(w_i) & \text{if } k = K + 1 \end{cases}$$

where $I(w_i = \ell_k)$ returns 1 if the token and the dish match, and 0 otherwise. We see that in order to prefer assigning customers to already occupied tables, we need $H_0(w)(Ka + b) < n_k - a$. Given $K \geq T$, and setting $H_0 = \frac{1}{T}$, we can approximate this with $\frac{1}{T}(Ta + b) < n_k - a$. From this we obtain $a < \frac{1}{2}(n_k - \frac{b}{T})$, which indicates that in order for tables with a single customer ($n_k = 1$) to attract further customers, a must be smaller than 0.5. Thus, there is a tension between the number of tables required by the data and our desire to reuse tables. One solution is to fix a to an arbitrary, sufficiently small value, as GGJ do in their experiments. In contrast, in this paper we infer a and b along with the other parameters, and change the other free variable, the base distribution H_0.

3 Morphology

The morphology model introduced by GGJ has a base distribution that generates not simply word types, as in the language model example, but morphological analyses. These are relatively simple, consisting of stem+suffix segmentation and a cluster membership. The probability of a word is the sum of the probability of all cluster c, stem s, suffix f tuples:

$$H_0(w) = \sum_{(c,s,f)} p(c) p(s|c) p(f|c) I(w = s.f) \tag{2}$$

with the stems and the suffixes being generated from cluster-specific distributions. In the GGJ model, all three distributions (cluster, stem, suffix) are finite conjugate symmetric Dirichlet-Multinomial (DirMult) distributions. We retain the DirMult over clusters, but change the morpheme-generating distributions.

The DirMult is equivalent to a Dirichlet Process prior (DP) with a finite base distribution; we use this representation because it allows us to replace the base distributions flexibly. A DP(α, H_0) is also equivalent to a PYP with $a = 0$, and thus also can be represented with a Chinese Restaurant Process, but in this case we sum over all tables to obtain the predictive probability of a (say) stem:

$$p(s|\alpha_s, H_S) = \frac{m_s + \alpha_s H_S}{\sum_{s'} m_{s'} + \alpha_s} \tag{3}$$

Note that the counts m_s refer to stems generated within the base distribution, not to token counts within the PYP.

The original GGJ model, ORIG, is equivalent to setting H_S for stems to $U(\frac{1}{S})$, and likewise $H_F = U(\frac{1}{F})$, where S and F are the number of possible stems and suffixes in the dataset (i.e., all possible prefix and suffix strings, including a null string).

There are two difficulties with this model. Firstly, it assumes a closed vocabulary and requires setting S and F in advance, by looking at the data. As a cognitive model, this is awkward, since it assumes a fixed, relatively small number of possible morphemes.

Secondly, when the PYP hyperparameters are inferred, a is set to be nearly 1, resulting in a model with as many tokens as tables. This behaviour is due to the interaction between vocabulary size and base distribution probabilities outlined in the previous section: this base distribution assigns relatively high probability to words, so new tables have high probability; as the number of tables increases (from its fairly large minimum), the optimal a for this table configuration also increases, resulting in convergence at the token-based model.

We investigate two alternate base distribution over stems and suffixes, both of which extend the space of possible morphemes, thereby lowering the overall probability of the observed words.

DP-CHAR generates morphemes by first generating a length $l \sim \text{Poisson}(\lambda)$. Characters are then drawn from a uniform distribution, $c_{0...l} \sim U(1/|\text{Chars}|)$. A morpheme's probability decreases exponentially by length, resulting in a strong preference for shorter morphemes.

DP-UNI simply extends the original uniform distribution to s and $f \sim U(1/1e6)$, in effect moving probability mass to a large number of unseen morphemes. It is thus similar to DP-CHAR without the length preference.

4 Inference

We follow the same inference procedure as GGJ, using Gibbs sampling. The sampler iterates between inferring each token's table assignment and resampling the table labels (see GGJ for details).

Within the morphology base distribution, the prior for the DirMult over clusters is set to $\alpha_k = 0.5$. To replicate the original DirMult model[1], we set $\alpha_s = 0.001S$ and $\alpha_f = 0.001F$. In the other models, $\alpha_s = \alpha_f = 1$. Within DP-CHAR, $\lambda = 6$ for stems, 0.5 for suffixes.

[1]In this model, the predictive posterior is defined as $p(s|\alpha, S) = \frac{m_s + \alpha}{m_. + S\alpha}$, using an alternate definition of α.

	Eve (Orth.)		Ornat (Orth.)	
	a	Tables/Type	a	Tables/Type
ORIG	0.96	21.2	0.97	10.64
DP-CHAR	0.46	1.4	0.56	1.17
DP-UNI	0.81	7.3	0.70	2.33

Table 1: Final values for a on the orthographic English and Spanish datasets, as well as the average number of tables for each word type. The 95% confidence interval across three runs is ≤ 0.01. (Phonological Eve is similar to Orthographic Eve.)

4.1 Sampling Hyperparameters

We sample PYP a and b hyperparameters using a slice sampler[2]. Previous work with this model has always fixed these values, generally finding small a to be optimal and b to have little effect. In experiments with fixed hyperparameters, we set $a = b = 0.1$.

To sample the hyperparameters, we place vague priors over them: $a \sim \text{Beta}(1, 1)$ and $b \sim \text{Gamma}(10, 0.1)$. The slice sampler samples a new value for a and b after every 10 iterations of Gibbs sampling.

5 Experiments

5.1 Datasets

Our datasets consist of the adult utterances from two morphologically annotated corpora from CHILDES, an English corpus, Eve (Brown, 1973), and a Spanish corpus, Ornat (Ornat, 1994). Morphology is marked by a grammatical suffix on the stem, e.g. *doggy*-PL. Words marked with irregular morphology are unsegmented.

The two languages, while related, have differing degrees of affixation: the English Eve corpus consists of 63 315 tokens (5% suffixed) and 1 988 types (28% suffixed); the Ornat corpus has 43 796 tokens (23% suffixed) and 3 157 types (50% suffixed). The English corpus has 17 gold suffix types, while Spanish has 72.

We also use the phonologically encoded Eve dataset used by GGJ. This dataset does not exactly correspond to the orthographic version, due to discrepancies in tokenisation, so we are unable to evaluate this dataset quantitatively.

[2]Mark Johnson's implementation, available at http://web.science.mq.edu.au/~mjohnson/Software.htm

	Eve (Orth.)			Ornat (Orth.)			Eve (Phon.)	
	% Seg	$\|L\|$	VM	% Seg	$\|L\|$	VM	% Seg	$\|L\|$
Gold	5			23			(5)	
ORIG Fix	7	1680	46.42(10.8)	14	2488	46.63(2.7)	17	1619
ORIG Inf	1	1893	9.94(1.0)	4	2769	17.80(3.7)	1	1984
DP-CHAR Fix	52	1331	15.33(0.3)	83	1828	35.76(1.1)	47	1289
DP-CHAR Inf	50	1330	16.15(0.4)	85	1824	36.47(0.5)	33	1317
DP-UNI Fix	38	1394	17.28(1.7)	51	1874	39.58(0.8)	36	1392
DP-UNI Inf	15	1574	31.54(3.1)	31	1983	42.48(1.1)	21	1500

Table 2: Final morphology results. 'Fix' refers to models with fixed PYP hyperparameters ($a = b = 0.1$), while 'Inf' models have inferred hyperparameters. % Seg shows the percentage of tokens that have a non-null suffix, while $|L|$ is the size of the morpheme lexicon. VM is shown with 95% confidence intervals.

5.2 Results

For each setting, we report the average over three runs of 1000 iterations of Gibbs sampling without annealing, using the last iteration for evaluation.

Table 1 shows what happens when hyperparameters are inferred: ORIG finds a token-based solution, with as many tables as tokens, while DP-CHAR is the opposite, with a small a allowing for just over one table for each word type. DP-UNI is between these two extremes. b is consistently between 1 and 3, confirming it has little effect.

The effect of the hyperparameters can be seen in the morphology results, shown in Table 2. DP-CHAR is robust across hyperparameter values, finding the same type-based solution with fixed and inferred hyperparameters, while the other models have very different results depending on the hyperparameter settings. ORIG with fixed hyperparameters performs best, with the highest VM score (a clustering measure, Rosenberg and Hirschberg (2007)) and a level of segmentation close to the correct one. However, with inferred hyperparameters, this model severely undersegments: it finds the unsegmented maximum likelihood solution, where all tokens are generated from the stem distribution (Goldwater, 2007).

The models with alternate base distributions go to the other extreme, oversegmenting the corpus. As generating new morphemes becomes less probable, the pressure to find the most compact morpheme lexicon grows. This leads to oversegmentation due to many spurious suffixes. The length penalty in DP-CHAR exacerbates this problem, but it can be seen in the DP-UNI solutions as well, particularly when hyperparameters are fixed to encourage a type-based solution.

6 Conclusion

The base distribution in the original GGJ model assigned a relatively high probability to unseen morphemes, allowing the model to generate new analyses for seen words instead of reusing old analyses and leading to undersegented token-based solutions. The alternative base distributions proposed here were effective in finding type-based solutions. However, these over-segmented solutions clearly do not match the true morphology, indicating that the model structure is inadequate.

One reason may be that the model structure is overly simple. The model is faced with an arguably more difficult task than a human learner, who has access to semantic, syntactic, and phonological cues. Adding these types of information has been shown to help morphology learning in similar models (Johnson, 2008b; Sirts and Goldwater, 2013; Frank et al., 2013).

Similarly, the morphological ambiguity that is captured by a model operating over tokens (and ignored in better-performing models that allow only a single analysis for each word type: Poon et al. (2009); Lee et al. (2011); Sirts and Alumäe (2012)) can often be disambiguated using semantic and syntactic information. A model that generates a single analysis per meaningful (semantically and syntactically distinct) word-form could avoid the potential problems of spurious re-generation seen in the original GGJ model as well as the converse problem of under-generation in our alternatives. Such a model might also map onto the human lexicon (which demonstrably avoids both problems) in a more realistic way.

References

Roger Brown. *A first language: The early stages*. Harvard University Press, Cambridge, MA, 1973.

Wray Buntine and Marcus Hutter. A Bayesian view of the Poisson-Dirichlet process. 2010. URL `arXiv:1007.0296`.

Joan Bybee. Regular morphology and the lexicon. *Language and Cognitive Processes*, 10: 425–455, 1995.

Stella Frank, Frank Keller, and Sharon Goldwater. Exploring the utility of joint morphological and syntactic learning from child-directed speech. In *Proceedings of the 18th Conference on Empirical Methods in Natural Language Processing (EMNLP)*, 2013.

Sharon Goldwater. *Nonparametric Bayesian Models of Lexical Acquisition*. PhD thesis, Brown University, 2007.

Sharon Goldwater, Thomas L. Griffiths, and Mark Johnson. Interpolating between types and tokens by estimating power-law generators. In *Advances in Neural Information Processing Systems 18*, 2006.

Sharon Goldwater, Thomas L. Griffiths, and Mark Johnson. Producing power-law distributions and damping word frequencies with two-stage language models. *Journal of Machine Learning Research*, 12:2335–2382, 2011.

Mark Johnson. Using Adaptor Grammars to identify synergies in the unsupervised acquisition of linguistic structure. In *Proceedings of the 46th Annual Meeting of the Association for Computational Linguistics (ACL)*, 2008a.

Mark Johnson. Unsupervised word segmentation for Sesotho using Adaptor Grammars. In *Proceedings of the Tenth Meeting of ACL Special Interest Group on Computational Morphology and Phonology*, pages 20–27, June 2008b.

Yoong Keok Lee, Aria Haghighi, and Regina Barzilay. Modeling syntactic context improves morphological segmentation. In *Proceedings of Fifteenth Conference on Computational Natural Language Learning (CONLL)*, 2011.

S. Lopez Ornat. *La adquisicion de la lengua espagnola*. Siglo XXI, Madrid, 1994.

Amy Perfors, Joshua B. Tenenbaum, and Terry Regier. The learnability of abstract syntactic principles. *Cognition*, 118(3):306 – 338, 2011.

Jim Pitman and Marc Yor. The two-parameter Poisson-Dirichlet distribution derived from a stable subordinator. *Annals of Probability*, 25 (2):855–900, 1997.

Hoifung Poon, Colin Cherry, and Kristina Toutanova. Unsupervised morphological segmentation with log-linear models. In *Proceedings of the Conference of the North American Chapter of the Association for Computational Linguistics (NAACL)*, 2009.

Andrew Rosenberg and Julia Hirschberg. V-measure: A conditional entropy-based external cluster evaluation measure. In *Proceedings of the 12th Conference on Empirical Methods in Natural Language Processing (EMNLP)*, 2007.

Kairit Sirts and Tanel Alumäe. A hierarchical Dirichlet process model for joint part-of-speech and morphology induction. In *Proceedings of the Conference of the North American Chapter of the Association for Computational Linguistics (NAACL)*, 2012.

Kairit Sirts and Sharon Goldwater. Minimally-supervised morphological segmentation using adaptor grammars. *Transactions of the Association for Computational Linguistics*, 1:231–242, 2013.

Yee Whye Teh. A hierarchical Bayesian language model based on Pitman-Yor processes. In *Proceedings of the 44th Annual Meeting of the Association for Computational Linguistics (ACL)*, Sydney, 2006.

An explicit statistical model of learning lexical segmentation using multiple cues

Çağrı Çöltekin
University of Groningen
c.coltekin@rug.nl

John Nerbonne
University of Groningen
j.nerbonne@rug.nl

Abstract

This paper presents an unsupervised and incremental model of learning segmentation that combines multiple cues whose use by children and adults were attested by experimental studies. The cues we exploit in this study are *predictability statistics*, *phonotactics*, *lexical stress* and partial *lexical information*. The performance of the model presented in this paper is competitive with the state-of-the-art segmentation models in the literature, while following the child language acquisition more faithfully. Besides the performance improvements over the similar models in the literature, the cues are combined in an explicit manner, allowing easier interpretation of what the model learns.

1 Introduction

Segmenting the continuous speech stream into lexical units is one of the challenges we face while listening to other speakers. For competent language users, probably the biggest aid in identifying the word boundaries is the knowledge of the words. Not surprisingly, the models of adult word recognition depend heavily on a lexicon (see Dahan and Magnuson, 2006, for a recent review). The same can be observed in speech and language technology where all automatic speech recognition systems make use of a comprehensive lexicon.

Even with a comprehensive lexicon and an error-free representation of the acoustic input, the problem is not trivial, since the input is often compatible with multiple segmentations spanning the complete utterance. The problem, however, is even more difficult for a learner who starts with no lexicon. Fortunately, the lexicon is not the only aid for segmentation. Experimental research within last two decades has revealed an array of cues that are used by adults and children for lexical segmentation. These cues include, but are not limited to, *lexical stress* (Cutler and Butterfield, 1992; Jusczyk, Houston, et al., 1999), *phonotactics* (Jusczyk, Cutler, et al., 1993), *predictability statistics* (Saffran et al., 1996), *allophonic differences* (Jusczyk, Hohne, et al., 1999), *coarticulation* (E. K. Johnson and Jusczyk, 2001), and *vowel harmony* (Suomi et al., 1997). The relative utility or dominance of these cues is a matter of current debate. However, it seems uncontroversial that none of these cues solves the segmentation problem alone and, when available, they are used in conjunction.

Along with experimental research on segmentation, a large number of computational models have been proposed in the literature. The early studies typically made use of connectionist models (e.g., Elman, 1990; Christiansen et al., 1998). Of these studies, Christiansen et al. (1998) is particularly interesting for the present study since it incorporates most of the cues used in this study. Using a simple recurrent network (SRN, Elman, 1990), Christiansen et al. (1998) demonstrated the usefulness of lexical stress, predictability statistics (included implicitly in any SRN model), and utterance boundaries, and showed that combining the cues improves the performance. The connectionist models have been instrumental in investigating a large number of cognitive phenomena. However, they have also been subject to the criticism that what a connectionist model learns is rather difficult to interpret. Furthermore, the performance achieved using connectionist models is far lower than that is expected from humans.

Models that use explicit representations in combination with statistical procedures (e.g., Brent and Cartwright, 1996; Brent, 1999; Venkataraman, 2001; Goldwater et al., 2009; M. Johnson and Goldwater, 2009) avoid both problems: these models perform better, and it is easier to reason about what they learn. Although these models were also instrumental in our understanding of the problem, they lack at least two aspects of connectionist models that fit human processing better. First, even though we know that human segmentation is incremental and predictive, most of these models process their input either in a batch fashion, or they require the complete utterance to be presented before attempting to segment the input. Second, it is generally difficult to incorporate arbitrary cues into most of these models.

Models that use explicit representations with incremental models exist (e.g., Monaghan and Christiansen, 2010; Lignos, 2011), but are rather rare. Furthermore, the investigation of cues and cue combination in segmentation is also relatively scarce within the recent studies (exceptions include the investigation of various suprevised models by Jarosz and J. A. Johnson, 2013).

The present paper introduces a strictly incremental, unsupervised method for learning segmentation where the learning method and internal representations are explicitly defined. Crucially, we use a set of cues demonstrated to be used by humans in solving the segmentation problem. The simulations results that we present are based on the same child-directed speech input used by many other studies in the literature.

The rest of this article is organized as follows: in the next section, we present a method for combining cues. Section 3 describes the cues used in this study. The simulations are described and results are presented in Section 4. A general discussion of the modeling framework and the simulation results are given in Section 5.

2 A cue combination method

We know that there is no single cue that always gives the correct answer in the lexical segmentation task. We also know that humans combine multiple cues when available. In this section we define a method to segment a given utterance using multiple boundary indicators, or cues, and learn to segment better by estimating usefulness of each indicator. In essence, each indicator makes a decision on each potential boundary location. The method combines these indicators' decisions to arrive at a hopefully more accurate decision. In machine learning terms, we formulate a number of binary classifiers, and aim to get a better classifier using a combination of them. This problems is a relatively well-studied subject in the machine learning literature (e.g., Bishop, 2006, chapter 14). Here a simple and well-known method, *majority voting*, will be used for combining multiple boundary indicators.

Majority voting is a common (and arguably effective) method in everyday social and political life. As a result, it has been well studied, and known to work well especially if each voter's decision is better than random on average, and votes are cast independently. In practice, even though the votes are almost never independent, majority voting is still an effective way of combining multiple classifiers (see Narasimhamurthy, 2005, for a discussion of the effectiveness of the method).

The majority voting combines each vote equally. Even though this may be a virtue in the social and political context, it is a shortcoming for a computational procedure that incorporates information from multiple sources with varying usefulness. We will use a simple augmentation of majority voting to model, *weighted majority voting* (Littlestone and Warmuth, 1994), that weighs the utility of the information provided by each source.

In weighted majority voting, the voters that make fewer errors get higher weights. In an unsupervised setting as ours, we do not know for certain when a voter makes an mistake. Instead, we take a voter's decision to be correct if it agrees with the majority. Initially we set all the weights to 1, trusting all the voters equally. We adopt an incremental version of the algorithm, where we keep the count of 'errors' made by each voter i, e_i, which is incremented every time the voter disagrees with the majority. After every boundary decision, first, the error counts are updated for each voter. Then, the weight, w_i, of each voter is updated using,

$$w_i \leftarrow 2\left(0.5 - \frac{e_i}{N}\right)$$

where N is the number of boundary decisions made so far, including the current one.

This update rule sets the weight of a voter that is half the time wrong (a voter that votes at random) to zero, eliminating the incompetent voters. If the votes of a voter are in accordance with the weighted majority decision almost all the time, the weight stays close to one.

3 Cues and boundary indicators

The combination method above allows us to combine an arbitrary number of boundary indicators. In our setting, each psychologically motivated cue is represented by multiple boundary indicators that differ based on the source of information used and the way this information is turned into a quantitative measure. This section introduces all of these cues, and the boundary indicators that stem from quantification of these cues in different ways.

3.1 Predictability statistics

At least as early as Harris (1955), it was known that a simple property of natural language utterances can aid identifying the lexical units that form an utterance: *predictability within the units is high, predictability between the units is low*. However, until the influential study by Saffran, Aslin, and Newport (1996), the idea was not investigated in developmental psycholinguistics as a possible source of information that children may use for segmentation. After Saffran et al. (1996) showed that 8-month-old infants make use of predictability statistics to extract word-like units from an artificial language stream, a large number of studies confirmed that predictability based strategies are used by adults and children for learning different aspects of language (e.g., Thiessen and Saffran, 2003; Newport and Aslin, 2004; Graf Estes et al., 2007; Thompson and Newport, 2007; Perruchet and Desaulty, 2008).

To use in our cue combination system, we need to quantify the notion of predictability. In this study, we use two information theoretic measures of predictability (or surprise), to define a set of boundary indicators. The first one, *pointwise mutual information* (MI) is defined as

$$\mathsf{MI}(l, r) = \log_2 \frac{\mathsf{P}(l, r)}{\mathsf{P}(l)\mathsf{P}(r)}$$

where l and r are strings of phonemes to the left and right of the possible boundary location. We define our second measure, *boundary entropy* (H) of a potential boundary after string l as

$$\mathsf{H}(l) = -\sum_{r \in A} \mathsf{P}(r|l) \log_2 (\mathsf{P}(r|l))$$

where the sum ranges over all phonemes in the alphabet, A.[1]

The use of both the MI and the H is motivated by the finding that combination multiple predictability measures result in better segmentation (see Çöltekin, 2011, p.101, for an analysis). Furthermore, for asymmetric measures, like entropy, $\mathsf{H}(l)$ is clearly not the same as $\mathsf{H}(r)$. Motivated by the finding that children use 'reverse predictability' (Pelucchi et al., 2009), we also incorporate a reverse entropy measure in the present study.

In most studies in the literature, the context l and r are single basic units (phonemes in our case). The different phoneme context sizes may capture regularities that exist because of different linguistic units. The relation between the phoneme context size and the linguistic units, of course, is not clear-cut. However, for example, we expect context size of one to capture the regularities between the phonemes, while context size of two or three to capture regularities between larger units, such as syllables.

The above parameters result in an array of indicators. However, none of the indicators we use have a natural threshold to decide whether a given position is a boundary or not. To get a boundary decision out of a single measure (MI or H), we adopt a method similar to a commonly used unsupervised method that decides for a boundary at the 'peaks' of unpredictability. A particular shortcoming of this strategy, however, is that it can never find both boundaries of a single-phoneme word, as there cannot be two peaks one after another. To remedy this, the *partial-peak* strategy we employ here makes use of two sets of boundary indicators for each potential boundary: one posits a boundary *after* an increase in H (or a decrease in MI) and the other posits a boundary *before* a decrease in H.

3.2 Utterance boundaries

An attractive aspect of the predictability-based segmentation is that it does not require any lexical knowledge in advance—unlike other cues noted in Section 1. However, certain aspects of phonotactics, such as the regularities found at the beginning and end of words, can be induced from the boundaries already marked in the input without the need for a lexicon. As a result, clearly marked lexical unit boundaries may serve as another source of information that can bootstrap the acquisition of lexical units.[2]

[1] The input to children is better represented by 'segments' or 'phones'. However, since the data used in our simulations does not contain any phonetic variation, in this paper, we use the term phoneme when referring to the basic input unit.

[2] There are a number of acoustic cues (e.g., pauses) that are highly correlated with lexical unit boundaries. However, we do not make use of them in this study since they are considered to be unreliable, and they are not marked in the corpora at hand.

All models of segmentation in the literature use utterance boundaries implicitly by assuming that the words cannot straddle utterance boundaries. The explicit use of utterance boundaries to discover regularities about words is common in connectionist models (e.g., Aslin et al., 1996; Christiansen et al., 1998; Stoianov and Nerbonne, 2000). Similar use of utterance boundaries in non-connectionist models is rather rare. Three exceptions to this are the models described by Brent (1996), Fleck (2008) and Monaghan and Christiansen (2010). The method described in this section is similar to Fleck's method, where the model estimates the probability of observing a boundary given its left and right context, $P(b|l,r)$, where b represents boundary, and as before, l and r represent left and right contexts, respectively. If this probability is greater than 0.5, the model inserts a boundary. Using utterance boundaries and the pauses, Fleck (2008) presents a batch algorithm with a few ad hoc corrections that estimates the probabilities $P(b), P(l|b), P(r|b), P(l), P(r)$, and uses Bayesian inversion to estimate $P(b|l,r)$.

In this work, instead of $P(b|l,r)$, we estimate probabilities of utterance beginnings, $P(ub|r)$, and probabilities of utterance ends, $P(ub|l)$, where ub stands for utterance boundary. These probabilities can directly be estimated from the utterance edges in the input corpus, and can be used as cues for discovering non-initial or non-final boundaries. Similar to the predictability, using different length l and r we obtain a set of indicators for $P(ub|r)$ and $P(ub|l)$.

Unlike $P(b|l,r)$, for $P(ub|r)$ and $P(ub|l)$ we do not have a straightforward threshold to make a boundary decision. Instead, we appeal to the familiar solution, and use 'partial peaks' in these values as boundary indications.

3.3 Lexical stress

Lexical stress is one of the cues for segmentation that is well supported by psycholinguistic research (e.g., Cutler and Butterfield, 1992; Jusczyk, Houston, et al., 1999; Jusczyk, 1999). Lexical stress is used in many languages for marking the prominent syllable in a word. For languages that exhibit lexical stress, the prominent syllable will typically be in a particular position in the word, allowing discovery of the boundaries based on the position of stressed syllable.

Despite the prominence of stress as a cue for segmentation, there are relatively few computational studies that investigate use of stress. Christiansen et al. (1998) incorporates stress as a cue in their connectionist cue combination system. Swingley (2005) provides a careful analysis of stress patterns of the bisyllabic words found by a discovery procedure on mutual information and frequency. Gambell and Yang (2006) present surprisingly good segmentation results with a rule-based learner whose main source of information is lexical stress. One of the major problems with the these studies, which has also been carried over to the present study, is the lack of corpora with realistic stress assignment (see Section 4.1).

Our stress-based strategy is similar to the strategy used for learning phonotactics described in Section 3.2. Instead of collecting statistics about phoneme n-grams, we collect statistics over stress assignments on phoneme n-grams. However, the probabilities are estimated over already known lexical units. Given stress patterns l and r, we estimate $P(b|l)$ from endings of the known lexical units, and $P(b|r)$ from the beginnings of the lexical units. Again we use these quantities as indicators for variable length l and r. Using the partial-peak boundary decision strategy in combination with the weighted majority voting algorithm, as before, we define a set of boundary indicators and operationalize lexical stress as another cue for segmentation.

3.4 Lexicon

For adults, a comprehensive lexicon is probably the most useful cue for segmentation. We do not expect infants to have a lexicon at the beginning. However, as they build their lexicon, or 'proto-lexicon', they may put it in use for discovering novel lexical units. This is the main strategy behind the majority of state-of-the-art computational models of segmentation (e.g., Brent, 1999; Venkataraman, 2001; Goldwater et al., 2009). The models that guess boundaries rarely build and use an explicit lexicon (exceptions include Monaghan and Christiansen, 2010).

In this study we also experiment with an (admittedly naive) set of lexical cues to word boundaries. The idea is to indicate a boundary when there are word-like strings on both sides of the boundary candidate. In our usual majority voting framework, these form two additional sets of boundary indicators. First, given a possible boundary location, we simply count the frequencies of already known words beginning or ending at the position in question. The second indicator is based on the number of times the phoneme sequences surrounding the boundary found at the beginnings or ends of the previously discovered words. The second indicator is essentially the same as the phonotactics component discussed in Section 3.2, except that it is calculated using already known word types instead of utterance boundaries.

Similar to the other asymmetric indicators discussed previously, we have two flavors for each indicator. One indicating the existence of words to the right of the boundary candidate (words beginning at the boundary), and the other indicating the existence of words the left of the boundary candidate (word ending at the boundary). As with the other cues, these result in a set of indicators whose primary source of information is the potential lexical units in the learner's incomplete and noisy lexicon.

4 Experiments

4.1 Data

We use a child-directed speech corpus from the CHILDES database (MacWhinney and Snow, 1985). It was collected by Bernstein Ratner (1987) and the original orthographic transcription of the corpus was converted to a phonemic transcription by Brent and Cartwright (1996). The same corpus has been used by many recent studies. Following the convention in the literature the corpus will be called the *BR corpus*.

For the results reported for segmentation strategies that make use of lexical stress, the BR corpus was marked for lexical stress semi-automatically following the procedure described by Christiansen et al. (1998) for annotating the Korman corpus (Korman, 1984). The stress assignment is done according to stress patterns in the MRC psycholinguistic database. All single-syllable words are coded as having primary stress, and the words that were not found or did not have stress assignment in the MRC database were annotated manually.

4.2 Evaluation metrics

Two quantitative measures, *precision* (P), *recall* (R) and their harmonic mean *F*$_1$*-score* (F-score, or F, for short), have become the standard evaluation measures for computational simulations. Following recent studies in the literature we present precision recall and F-scores for boundaries (BP, BR, BF), word tokens (WP, WR, WF) and word types or lexicon (LP, LR, LF). Besides precision and recall, we also present two error measures, oversegmentation (E_o) and undersegmentation (E_u) errors, defined as $E_o = FP/(FP + TN)$ and $E_u = FN/(FN + TP)$, where TP, FP, TN and FN are true positives, false positives, true negatives, and false negatives respectively.

In plain words, E_o is the number of the false boundaries inserted by the model divided by the total number of word internal positions in the corpus. Similarly, E_u is the ratio of boundaries missed to the total number of boundaries. Although these error measures are related to precision and recall, they provide different, and sometimes better, insights into the model's behavior.

4.3 Reference models

In this paper, we compare the results obtained by the cue combination model with two baselines. The first baseline is a random model (RM) that assigns boundaries with the probability of boundaries in the input corpus. The RM is more informed than a completely random classifier, but it has been customary (since Brent and Cartwright, 1996) in segmentation literature to set the bar a little bit higher. The second reference model is a lexicon-building model similar to many state-of-the-art models. The model described here, which we call LM, assigns probabilities to possible segmentations as described in Equations 1 and 2.

$$P(s) = \prod_{i=1}^{n} P(w_i) \tag{1}$$

$$P(w) = \begin{cases} (1-\alpha)f(w) & \text{if } w \text{ is known} \\ \alpha \prod_{i=1}^{m} P(a_i) & \text{if } w \text{ is unknown} \end{cases} \tag{2}$$

where s is a sequence of phonemes (e.g., an utterance or a corpus), w_i is the ith word in the sequence, a_i is the ith sound in the word, $f(w)$ is the relative frequency of the word w, m is the number of known words, and $0 \leq \alpha \leq 1$ is the only parameter of the model. In all experiments reported in this paper, we will fix α at 0.5.

For the incremental model defined here, a word is 'known', if it was used in a previous segmentation. The model accepts whole utterances as single words if the utterance does not contain any known words.

	boundary			word			lexicon		
model	P	R	F	P	R	F	P	R	F
Brent (1999)	80.3	84.3	82.3	67.0	69.4	68.2	53.6	51.3	52.4
Venkataraman (2001)	81.7	82.5	82.1	68.1	68.6	68.3	54.5	57.0	55.7
Goldwater et al. (2009)	90.3	80.8	85.2	75.2	69.6	72.3	63.5	55.2	59.1
Blanchard et al. (2010)	81.4	82.5	81.9	65.8	66.4	66.1	57.2	55.4	56.3
RM	27.4	27.0	27.2	12.6	12.5	12.5	6.0	43.6	10.5
LM	84.1	82.7	83.4	72.0	71.2	71.6	50.6	61.0	55.3

Table 1: Performance scores of the reference models LM and RM in comparison with some of the earlier scores reported in the literature. If there were multiple models reported in a study, the result with the highest lexicon F-score is presented. All scores are obtained on the BR corpus.

Table 1 compares the performances of some recent models in the literature using the BR corpus with the two reference models. The LM performs similar to the state-of-the-art models presented in this table. Hence, to aid comparison of the models proposed in this study with the others in the literature, we will (re)report the result of the two baseline models in the rest of this paper. Note that the scores presented in Table 1 can be misleading since the batch models have an advantage due to the way scores are calculated. The scores of the batch models are calculated at the end of training, while scores of the incremental models include initial (presumably bad) choices made before enough exposure to the input. For example, the LM achieves boundary, word and lexicon F-scores of 89%, 81% and 74% respectively, towards the end of the BR corpus. These scores are higher than all of the scores presented in Table 1 (see Table 4 for details the way these scores are calculated).

4.4 Experiments and results

This section reports results of a set of simulations using the modeling framework described so far. All experiments are run on the BR corpus. For all the results reported below, each cue is represented by a set indicators as described in Section 3, multiple indicators for each phoneme n-gram of length one and three are used for left (l) and right (r) contexts, for all measures that are calculated over phoneme n-grams surrounding the potential boundary. The use of lexical information and lexical stress as standalone strategies are similar to the 'lexicon-building' strategy. The learner inserts complete utterances to the lexicon when the strategy cannot segment the utterance. As the learner starts to learn (from the edges of the sequences in the lexicon) what the edges of words look like, it uses this information to segment later utterances in the input.[3]

We first report the performance results of individual cues, namely, *predictability* (P), *utterance boundaries* (U), *lexical information* (W) and *lexical stress* (S) in Table 2.

Using the predictability cue alone leads to a segmentation performance lower than but close to the state-of-the-art reference model LM. Although these results are not directly comparable to the earlier studies in the literature, the performance scores presented in Table 2 are the best scores presented to date for models using the predictability cue alone. Graphs presented by Brent (1999) indicates about 50%–60% WP and WR and 20%–30% LP for his baseline model utilizing mutual information on the BR corpus. Cohen et al. (2007) report 76% BP, and 75% BR on George Orwell's 1984. Christiansen et al. (1998) report 37% WP and 40% WR with an SRN using phonotactics and utterance boundary cues on another child-directed speech corpus (Korman, 1984).

The model that learns from the utterance boundaries seems to perform the best. The results are comparable, and in some cases better than the LM. Furthermore, the overall scores are also higher than the scores reported by Fleck (2008), where the boundary, word and lexical F-scores were 82.9%, 70.7% and 36.6%, respectively.

Although it is somewhat behind both predictability and utterance boundary cues, the lexical information alone certainly performs better than random. The lower performance of this model in comparison to 'U' suggests that, at least in this setting, phonotactics learned from word tokens found at the utterance edges leads to a better performance compared to the phonotactics learned from the word types in the learner's lexicon.

The experiment that takes only the stress cue into account yields the worst overall results. It seems, when the cue indicates a boundary, it is extremely precise. However, it is also very conservative. This seems to be due to the fact that the model learns to segment at weak–strong transitions, which is expected to be precise. However, since majority of the stress transitions are strong–strong, this covers rather a small portion of the boundaries.

[3]The source code of the application and the data used in this study can be found at `https://bitbucket.org/coltekin/seg/`.

	boundary			word			lexicon			error	
model	P	R	F	P	R	F	P	R	F	E_o	E_u
P	69.6	92.5	79.5	56.9	70.2	62.9	36.7	49.8	42.3	15.3	7.5
U	82.9	84.8	83.8	70.5	71.7	71.1	33.8	66.9	44.9	6.6	15.2
W	77.5	71.3	74.3	60.6	57.2	58.9	18.3	47.7	26.4	7.8	28.7
S	78.2	8.2	14.8	26.5	9.7	14.2	8.2	38.7	13.5	0.9	92.8
RM	27.4	27.0	27.2	12.6	12.5	12.5	6.0	43.6	10.5	27.1	73.0
LM	84.1	82.7	83.4	72.0	71.2	71.6	50.6	61.0	55.3	5.9	17.3

Table 2: Results of simulations using individual cues: predictability (P), utterance boundaries (U), lexicon (W) and lexical stress (S). The rows labeled LM and RM are scores of reference models repeated for ease of comparison.

	boundary			word			lexicon			error	
model	P	R	F	P	R	F	P	R	F	E_o	E_u
PU	82.6	90.7	86.5	72.4	77.4	74.8	42.8	65.3	51.7	7.2	9.3
PUW	83.7	91.2	87.3	74.1	78.8	76.4	43.9	67.7	53.3	6.7	8.8
PUWS	92.8	75.7	83.4	78.3	68.1	72.9	26.8	62.7	37.5	2.2	24.3
RM	27.4	27.0	27.2	12.6	12.5	12.5	6.0	43.6	10.5	27.1	73.0
LM	84.1	82.7	83.4	72.0	71.2	71.6	50.6	61.0	55.3	5.9	17.3

Table 3: Results of combination of strategies based on four cues: starting with predictability and utterance boundaries (PU), addition of lexicon (PUW) and lexical stress (PUWS). The rows labeled LM and RM are scores of reference models repeated for ease of comparison.

Table 3 presents combination of predictability and utterance boundaries, followed by lexical information and stress. Here all indicators are combined in a flat, non-hierarchical manner. The combination of predictability and utterance boundaries results in higher F-scores, and it results in more balanced under- and over-segmentation errors. The addition of the lexical information provide a small but consistent improvement. However, adding stress information seems to have an adverse effect. Despite the increased boundary and word precision, all other performance scores go down substantially when we add the stress cue.

The scores in Table 3 are obtained over the complete corpus. As noted in Section 4.3, these scores do not reflect the 'learned' state of the models. Furthermore, we are interested in the progress of a learner as more input is provided. To demonstrate both, E_o and E_u for all combined models are plotted in Figure 1 for each 500 utterances.

An interesting observation that can be made in these graphs is that the models without the stress cue make fewer undersegmentation errors, with the cost of slightly higher oversegmentation. However, the strategy that combines all cues keeps

	boundary			word			lexicon			error	
model	P	R	F	P	R	F	P	R	F	E_o	E_u
PU	85.6	96.7	90.8	78.7	86.0	82.2	71.8	75.9	73.8	6.6	3.3
PUW	83.3	97.2	89.7	75.6	84.5	79.8	69.8	75.5	72.5	7.9	2.8
PUWS	92.5	89.3	90.9	84.2	82.2	83.2	70.9	77.6	74.1	2.9	10.7

Table 4: The same results presented in Table 3, but measured for the last 290-utterances (last block in an incremental experiment with 500-utterance increments).

oversegmentation errors low throughout the learning process, and towards the end, it makes fewer undersegmentation errors as well. This suggests that the model combining all cues, including the stress, may be doing better as it collects more evidence. To demonstrate this further, Table 4 presents the same results presented in Table 3, calculated on the last block of an experiment where performance scores were calculated after every 500 input utterances. Besides demonstrating the increase in performance scores when calculated at later stages of learning, the differences between tables 3 and 4 show clearly that despite the fact that it has a detrimental affect when scores are calculated over the complete corpus, the stress cue has a positive effect at the end of the learning process. This suggests that the combined model using stress cue learns slower and makes more mistakes at the beginning. However as evidence accumulates, it starts to be useful, and increases the overall performance of the combined model.

5 General discussion

This paper introduced an unsupervised and incremental model of segmentation that focuses on combining multiple cues relevant to child language acquisition as attested by earlier studies in psycholinguistics. Unsupervised and incremental models of segmentation that combine multiple cues are not new. There have been many models sharing these properties to some extent. In particular, the model presented in this paper has many similarities with an earlier connectionist model of segmentation presented by Christiansen et al. (1998). However, unlike connectionist models, the model presented here uses accessible explicit representations, and an concrete learning procedure.

Most recent models with explicit representations and statistical learning procedures tend to be models that process their input in 'batch'. These models typically perform better when measured at the overall best performance level, and the insights

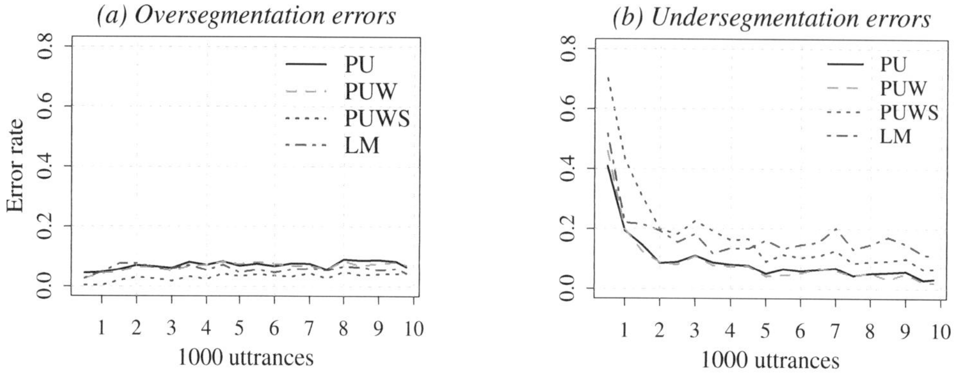

Figure 1: Progression of (a) over- and (b) under-segmentation errors of the combined strategies.

we get from these models are undeniably useful. However, these models typically provide explanations at Marr's (1982) *computational level*. The modeling practice we follow is similar to these models in many ways, and can provide explanations for the same type of questions. However, it may also provide explanations at lower levels (e.g., Marr's *algorithmic level*). This is not to claim that children learn exactly the way the model learns. However, the type of models presented in this paper follow human behavior more faithfully, and, at least in principle, more detailed predictions can be tested on these models. Naturally, relevance of the findings for human cognition will be increased as we constrain our models further in accordance with what we know about the cognitive processes.

The first contribution of this study is the description of a modeling framework that follows what we know about human segmentation process with high fidelity while keeping the benefits of a model with explicit representations and statistical learning methods.

Besides the performance scores that are competitive with the state-of-the-art models in the literature, the simulations also provide some insights regarding the cues commonly studied in the psycholinguistics literature. Some of the findings confirm the previous results. Indeed, it seems that combining multiple cues help. However, the properties of the modeling framework presented in this paper allows us to make some other interesting observations, for example, the effect of stress cue presented in Section 4.4.

When we look at the overall effect of the stress cue throughout the complete simulations, it seems stress degrades the performance. However, if we take a look at the models' performances at the end of the learning, we see that effect of the stress cue is actually positive. In other words, once 'bootstrapped' by the other cues, stress becomes a useful cue. Furthermore, the way the stress cue is useful for the model is also in line with the findings in the literature where stress is commonly found to be a dominant cue (Jusczyk, Cutler, et al., 1993; Thiessen and Saffran, 2003). Given the findings here that stress is rather a precise cue (despite its low recall), it is understandable why it dominates the boundary decisions when available.

The segmentation model presented in this paper demonstrates a way to achieve good segmentation performance using more cognitively relevant and transparent strategies. It is also instrumental at investigating some of the interesting issues regarding cue combination in segmentation, and it is a first step towards models that are more faithful to the human segmentation process. Among other things, we consider two important improvements to the model described here for future work. First, although the combination method used (weighted majority voting) has been successful, other methods such as Bayesian cue combination used for modeling other cognitive processes may be a better approach for segmentation as well. The second improvement we plan is regarding the input. Even though we used a standard corpus as used by many other studies in the literature, it is idealized (e.g., contains no phonetic variation), and poor (e.g., lacking some cues that are available to children) at the same time. Hence, as well as better input representations, using input with variation and noise, and the use of different languages are steps we would like to take in future studies towards a better modeling of segmentation.

References

Richard N. Aslin, Julide Z. Woodward, Nicholas P. LaMendola, and Thomas G. Bever (1996). "Models of Word Segmentation in Fluent Maternal Speech to Infants". In: *Signal to Syntax: Bootstrapping From Speech to Grammar in Early Acquisition.* Ed. by James L. Morgan and Katherine Demuth. Lawrence Erlbaum Associates. Chap. 8, pp. 117–134.

Nan Bernstein Ratner (1987). "The phonology of parent-child speech". In: *Children's language.* Ed. by K. Nelson and A. van Kleeck. Vol. 6. Hillsdale, NJ: Erlbaum, pp. 159–174.

Christopher M. Bishop (2006). *Pattern Recognition and Machine Learning.* Springer.

Daniel Blanchard, Jeffrey Heinz, and Roberta Golinkoff (2010). "Modeling the contribution of phonotactic cues to the problem of word segmentation". In: *Journal of Child Language* 37.Special Issue 03, pp. 487–511.

Michael R. Brent (1996). "Advances in the computational study of language acquisition". In: *Cognition* 61 (1-2), pp. 1–38.

Michael R. Brent (1999). "An Efficient, Probabilistically Sound Algorithm for Segmentation and Word Discovery". In: *Machine Learning* 34.1-3, pp. 71–105.

Michael R. Brent and Timothy A. Cartwright (1996). "Distributional regularity and phonotactic constraints are useful for segmentation". In: *Cognition* 61 (1-2), pp. 93–125.

Morten H. Christiansen, Joseph Allen, and Mark S. Seidenberg (1998). "Learning to Segment Speech Using Multiple Cues: A Connectionist Model". In: *Language and Cognitive Processes* 13.2, pp. 221–268.

Paul Cohen, Niall Adams, and Brent Heeringa (2007). "Voting experts: An unsupervised algorithm for segmenting sequences". In: *Intelligent Data Analysis* 11.6, pp. 607–625.

Çağrı Çöltekin (2011). "Catching Words in a Stream of Speech: Computational simulations of segmenting transcribed child-directed speech". PhD thesis. University of Groningen.

Anne Cutler and Sally Butterfield (1992). "Rhythmic cues to speech segmentation: Evidence from juncture misperception". In: *Journal of Memory and Language* 31.2, pp. 218–236.

Delphine Dahan and James S. Magnuson (2006). "Spoken Word Recognition". In: *Handbook of Psycholinguistics.* 2nd. Elsevier. Chap. 8, pp. 249–283.

Jeffrey L. Elman (1990). "Finding Structure in Time". In: *Cognitive Science* 14, pp. 179–211.

Margaret M. Fleck (2008). "Lexicalized phonotactic word segmentation". In: *Proceedings of the Annual Meeting of the Association of Computational Linguistics (ACL-08)*, pp. 130–138.

Timothy Gambell and Charles Yang (2006). *Word segmentation: Quick but not dirty.* Unpublished manuscript.

Sharon Goldwater, Thomas L. Griffiths, and Mark Johnson (2009). "A Bayesian framework for word segmentation: Exploring the effects of context". In: *Cognition* 112 (1), pp. 21–54.

Katharine Graf Estes, Julia L. Evans, Martha W. Alibali, and Jenny R. Saffran (2007). "Can Infants Map Meaning to Newly Segmented Words? Statistical Segmentation and Word Learning". In: *Psychological Science* 18.3, pp. 254–260.

Zellig S. Harris (1955). "From Phoneme to Morpheme". In: *Language* 31.2, pp. 190–222.

Gaja Jarosz and J. Alex Johnson (2013). "The Richness of Distributional Cues to Word Boundaries in Speech to Young Children". In: *Language Learning and Development* 9.2, pp. 175–210.

Elizabeth K. Johnson and Peter W. Jusczyk (2001). "Word Segmentation by 8-Month-Olds: When Speech Cues Count More Than Statistics". In: *Journal of Memory and Language* 44.4, pp. 548–567.

Mark Johnson and Sharon Goldwater (2009). "Improving nonparameteric Bayesian inference: experiments on unsupervised word segmentation with adaptor grammars". In: *Proceedings of Human Language Technologies: The 2009 Annual Conference of the North American Chapter of the Association for Computational Linguistics*, pp. 317–325.

Peter W. Jusczyk (1999). "How infants begin to extract words from speech". In: *Trends in Cognitive Sciences* 3.9, pp. 323–328.

Peter W. Jusczyk, Anne Cutler, and Nancy J. Redanz (1993). "Infants' preference for the predominant stress patterns of English words". In: *Child Development* 64.3, pp. 675–687.

Peter W. Jusczyk, Elizabeth A. Hohne, and Angela Bauman (1999). "Infants' sensitivity to allophonic cues for word segmentation". In: *Perception and Psychophysics* 61.8, pp. 1465–1476.

Peter W. Jusczyk, Derek M. Houston, and Mary Newsome (1999). "The Beginnings of Word Segmentation in English-Learning Infants". In: *Cognitive Psychology* 39, pp. 159–207.

Myron Korman (1984). "Adaptive aspects of maternal vocalizations in differing contexts at ten weeks". In: *First Language* 5, pp. 44–45.

Constantine Lignos (2011). "Modeling infant word segmentation". In: *Proceedings of the Fifteenth Conference on Computational Natural Language Learning*, pp. 29–38.

Nick Littlestone and Manfred K. Warmuth (1994). "The Weighted Majority Algorithm". In: *Information and Computation* 108.2, pp. 212–261.

Brian MacWhinney and Catherine Snow (1985). "The child language data exchange system". In: *Journal of Child Language* 12.2, pp. 271–269.

David Marr (1982). *Vision: A Computational Investigation into the Human Representation and Processing of Visual Information.* New York: Freeman.

Padraic Monaghan and Morten H. Christiansen (2010). "Words in puddles of sound: modelling psycholinguistic effects in speech segmentation". In: *Journal of Child Language* 37.Special Issue 03, pp. 545–564.

Anand Narasimhamurthy (2005). "Theoretical Bounds of Majority Voting Performance for a Binary Classification Problem". In: *IEEE Trans. Pattern Anal. Mach. Intell.* 27 (12), pp. 1988–1995.

Elissa L. Newport and Richard N. Aslin (2004). "Learning at a distance: I. Statistical learning of non-adjacent dependencies". In: *Cognitive Psychology* 48.2, pp. 127–162.

Bruna Pelucchi, Jessica F. Hay, and Jenny R. Saffran (2009). "Learning in reverse: Eight-month-old infants track backward transitional probabilities". In: *Cognition* 113.2, pp. 244–247.

Pierre Perruchet and Stéphane Desaulty (2008). "A role for backward transitional probabilities in word segmentation?" In: *Memory and Cognition* 36.7, pp. 1299–1305.

Jenny R. Saffran, Richard N. Aslin, and Elissa L. Newport (1996). "Statistical learning by 8-month old infants". In: *Science* 274.5294, pp. 1926–1928.

Ivelin Stoianov and John Nerbonne (2000). "Exploring Phonotactics with Simple Recurrent Networks". In: *Proceedings of Computational Linguistics in the Netherlands 1999.* Ed. by Frank van Eynde, Ineke Schuurman, and Ness Schelkens, pp. 51–67.

Kari Suomi, James M. McQueen, and Anne Cutler (1997). "Vowel Harmony and Speech Segmentation in Finnish". In: *Journal of Memory and Language* 36.3, pp. 422–444.

Daniel Swingley (2005). "Statistical clustering and the contents of the infant vocabulary". In: *Cognitive Psychology* 50.1, pp. 86–132.

Erik D. Thiessen and Jenny R. Saffran (2003). "When Cues Collide: Use of Stress and Statistical Cues to Word Boundaries by 7- to 9-Month-Old Infants," in: *Developmental Psychology* 39.4, pp. 706–716.

Susan P. Thompson and Elissa L. Newport (2007). "Statistical Learning of Syntax: The Role of Transitional Probability". In: *Language Learning and Development* 3.1, pp. 1–42.

Anand Venkataraman (2001). "A Statistical Model for Word Discovery in Transcribed Speech". In: *Computational Linguistics* 27.3, pp. 351–372.

Distributional Learning as a Theory of Language Acquisition (Extended Abstract)

Alexander Clark
Department of Philosophy
King's College, London
Strand, London
alexander.clark@kcl.ac.uk

1 Abstract

In recent years, a theory of distributional learning of phrase structure grammars has been developed starting with the simple algorithm presented in (Clark and Eyraud, 2007). These ideas are based on the classic ideas of American structuralist linguistics (Wells, 1947; Harris, 1954). Since that initial paper, the algorithms have been extended to large classes of grammars, notably to the class of Multiple Context-Free grammars by (Yoshinaka, 2011).

In this talk we will sketch a theory of language acquisition based on these techniques, and contrast it with other proposals, such as the semantic bootstrapping and parameter setting models. This proposal is based on three recent results: first, a weak learning result for a class of languages that plausibly includes all natural languages (Clark and Yoshinaka, 2013), secondly, a strong learning result for some context-free grammars, that includes a general strategy for converting weak learners to strong learners (Clark, 2013a), and finally a theoretical result that all minimal grammars for a language will have distributionally definable syntactic categories (Clark, 2013b). We argue that we now have all of the pieces for a complete and explanatory theory of language acquisition based on distributional learning and sketch some of the non-trivial predictions of this theory about the syntax and syntax-semantics interface.

2 Biography

Alexander Clark is a Lecturer in Logic and Linguistics in the Department of Philosophy at King's College London; before that he taught for several years in the Computer Science department of Royal Holloway, University of London. His first degree was in Mathematics from the University of Cambridge, and his Ph.D. is from the University of Sussex. He did postdoctoral research at the University of Geneva. He is currently President of SIGNLL and chair of the steering committee of the International Conference on Grammatical Inference. His research is on unsupervised learning in computational linguistics, grammatical inference, and theoretical and mathematical linguistics.

References

Alexander Clark and Rémi Eyraud. 2007. Polynomial identification in the limit of substitutable context-free languages. *Journal of Machine Learning Research*, 8:1725–1745, August.

Alexander Clark and Ryo Yoshinaka. 2013. Distributional learning of parallel multiple context-free grammars. *Machine Learning*, pages 1–27.

Alexander Clark. 2013a. Learning trees from strings: A strong learning algorithm for some context-free grammars. *Journal of Machine Learning Research*, 14:3537–3559.

Alexander Clark. 2013b. The syntactic concept lattice: Another algebraic theory of the context-free languages? *Journal of Logic and Computation*.

Zellig Harris. 1954. Distributional structure. *Word*, 10(2-3):146–62.

R. S. Wells. 1947. Immediate constituents. *Language*, 23(2):81–117.

R. Yoshinaka. 2011. Efficient learning of multiple context-free languages with multidimensional substitutability from positive data. *Theoretical Computer Science*, 412(19):1821 – 1831.

A multimodal corpus for the evaluation of computational models for (grounded) language acquisition

Judith Gaspers[a], Maximilian Panzner[a], Andre Lemme[b], Philipp Cimiano[a], Katharina J. Rohlfing[c], Sebastian Wrede[b]

[a]Semantic Computing Group, CITEC, Bielefeld University, Germany
{jgaspers|mpanzner|cimiano}@cit-ec.uni-bielefeld.de
[b]Research Institute for Cognition and Robotics (CoR-Lab), Bielefeld University, Germany
{alemme|swrede}@cor-lab.uni-bielefeld.de
[c]Emergentist Semantics Group, CITEC, Bielefeld University, Germany
kjr@uni-bielefeld.de

Abstract

This paper describes the design and acquisition of a German multimodal corpus for the development and evaluation of computational models for (grounded) language acquisition and algorithms enabling corresponding capabilities in robots. The corpus contains parallel data from multiple speakers/actors, including speech, visual data from different perspectives and body posture data. The corpus is designed to support the development and evaluation of models learning rather complex grounded linguistic structures, e.g. syntactic patterns, from sub-symbolic input. It provides moreover a valuable resource for evaluating algorithms addressing several other learning processes, e.g. concept formation or acquisition of manipulation skills. The corpus will be made available to the public.

1 Introduction

Children acquire linguistic structures through exposure to (spoken) language in a rich context and environment. The semantics of language may be learned by establishing connections between linguistic structures and corresponding structures in the environment, i.e. in different domains such as the visual one (Harnad, 1990). Both with respect to modeling language acquisition in children and with respect to enabling corresponding language acquisition capabilities in robots, which may ideally be also grounded in their environment, it is hence of great interest to explore i) how linguistic structures of different levels of complexity, e.g. words or grammatical phrases, can be derived from speech input, ii) how structured representations for entities observed in the environment can be derived, e.g. how concepts and structured representations of actions can be formed, and iii) how connections can be established between structured representations derived from different domains. In order to gain insights concerning the mechanisms at play during language acquisition (LA), which enable children to solve these learning tasks, models are needed which ideally cover several learning tasks. For instance, they may cover the acquisition of both words and grammatical rules as well as the acquisition of their grounded meanings. Complementarily, data resources are needed which enable the design and evaluation of these models by providing suitable parallel data.

Aiming to provide a basis for the development and evaluation of LA models addressing the acquisition of rather complex and grounded linguistic structures, i.e. syntactic patterns, from sub-symbolic input, we designed a German multimodal input corpus. The corpus consists of data of multiple speakers/actors who performed actions in front of a robot and described these actions while executing them. Subjects were recorded, i.e. parallel data of speech, stereo vision (including the view-perspective of the "infant"/robot) and body postures were gathered. The resulting data hence allow grounding of linguistic structures in both vision and body postures. Among others, learning processes that may be evaluated using the corpus include: acquisition of several linguistic structures, acquisition of visual structures, concept formation, acquisition of generalized patterns which abstract over different speakers and actors, establishment of correspondences between structures from different domains, acquisition of manipulation skills, and development of appropriate models for the representations of actions.

This paper is organized as follows. Next, we will provide background information concerning computational models of LA. In Section 3, we will then describe the corpus design and acquisition, including the desired properties of the collected data, corresponding experimental settings and technical implementation. We will then present the resulting data set and subsequently conclude..

2 Background

To date, several models addressing LA learning tasks have been proposed and evaluated using different copora. Yet, these models typically focus on a subset or certain aspects of the LA learning tasks mentioned in the previous section, often assuming other learning tasks, e.g. those of lower complexity, as already solved by the learner. For instance, models addressing the acquisition of grammatical constructions and their meaning (Kwiatkowski et al., 2012; Alishahi and Stevenson, 2008; Gaspers and Cimiano, in press; Chang and Maia, 2001) typically learn from symbolic input. In particular, assuming that the child is already able to segment a speech signal into a stream of words and to extract structured representations from the visual context, such models typically explore learning from sequences of words and symbolic descriptions of the non-linguistic context. Models addressing the acquisition of word-like units directly from a speech signal (Räsänen, 2011; Räsänen et al., 2009) have also been explored. These, however, typically do not address learning of more complex linguistic structures/constructions.

Taken together, lexical acquisition from speech and syntactic acquisition have been mainly studied independently of each other, often assuming that syntactic acquisition follows from knowledge of words. However, learning processes might actually be interleaved, and top-down learning processes may play an important role in LA. For instance, with respect to computational learning from symbolic input, it has been shown that knowledge of syntax can facilitate word learning (Yu, 2006). Children may, for instance, also make use of syntactic cues during speech segmentation and/or word learning, but models addressing lexical acquisition from speech have to date mainly ignored syntax (Räsänen, 2012). Models addressing the acquisition of syntactic patterns directly from speech provide a basis for exploring to what extent learning mechanisms might be interleaved in early LA. Moreover, they allow to investigate the possible role of several top-down learning processes which have to date been little explored.

Several corpora comprising interactions of children with their caregivers have been collected. A large such resource is the CHILDES data base (MacWhinney, 2000), which contains transcribed speech. Data from CHILDES have been often used to evaluate models learning from symbolic input, in particular models for syntactic acquisition from sequences of words; additional accompanying symbolic context representations have been often created (semi–)automatically. Moreover, multimodal corpora containing caregiver-child interactions have been recorded and annotated (Björkenstam and Wirn, 2013; Yu et al., 2008), thus also allowing to study the role of social interaction and extra-linguistic cues in language learning. By contrast, in this work we aim to provide a basis for developing and evaluating models which address the acquisition of syntactic patterns from speech. Hence, allowing to derive generalized patterns, linguistic units as well as the objects and actions they refer to have to re-appear in the data several times. Thus, in line with the CAREGIVER corpus (Altosaar et al., 2010) we did not record caregiver-child interactions but attempted to approximate speech used by caregivers with respect to the learning task(s) at hand. However, the focus of the CAREGIVER corpus is on models learning word-like units from speech. Thus, a number of keywords were spoken in different carrier sentences; speech is accompanied by only limited non-linguistic context information in the corpus. In contrast to CAREGIVER, we did not restrict language use directly and recorded parallel context information from different modalities, focusing not only on the acquisition of word-like units from speech and word-to-object mapping but moreover on the acquisition of simple syntactic patterns and mapping language to actions.

3 Corpus design and acquisition

In this section, we will first describe the desired properties of the corpus. Subsequently, we will present the corresponding experimental settings, used stimuli and procedure, the technical implementation of the robot behavior and the data acquisition as well as the resulting corpus.

3.1 Desired properties

Our goal was to design a corpus comprising multimodal data which supports the evaluation of computational models addressing several LA learning tasks, and in particular the acquisition of grounded syntactic patterns from sub-symbolic input only as well as the development of components supporting the acquisition of language by robots. Thus, the main focus was to design the corpus in such a way that the data acquisition scenario was simplified enough to allow solving the task of learning grounded syntactic patterns from sub-symbolic input with the resulting data set (which of course contains much less data when compared to the innumerable natural language examples children receive when acquiring language over several years). In particular, since the acquisition of rather complex structures should be enabled using sub-symbolic information, several (repeated) examples for contained structures were needed, allowing the formation of generalized representations. Thus, we opted for a rather simple scenario. Specifically, the following properties were taken into account:

- Rather few objects and actions were included that could moreover be differentiated rather easily from a visual point of view. However, in order to reflect differences between actions, these differed i) with respect to the number of their referents as well as ii) with respect to their specificity to certain objects. In particular, we included actions which could be performed on different subsets of the objects, ranging from specificity to one certain object to being executed with all of the objects.

- Objects and actions reappeared several times, yielding several examples for each of them. Repeated appearance is an essential aspect, since the formation of generalized representations starting from continuous input requires several observations in order to allow abstraction over observed examples/different actors and speakers.

- The scenario was designed such that it encouraged human subjects to use rather simple syntactic patterns/short sentences. Yet, language use was in principle unrestricted in order to acquire rather natural data and to capture speaker-dependent differences. This also reflects the input children receive in that parents use rather simple language when talking to children.

- Data were gathered from several human subjects in order to allow for the evaluation of generalization over different speakers (with different acoustic properties and different language use, e.g. different words for objects, different syntactic patterns with different complexity, etc) as well as over different actors in case of actions, since children interact with different people and are able to solve this task. Moreover, generalization to different speakers/actors is also important with respect to learning in artificial agents which should preferably not be operable by a single person only.

- Parallel data were gathered in which objects and actions were explicitly named when they were used. This is an important aspect because the corpus should allow learning connections between vision, i.e. objects and actions, and speech (segments) referring to these objects/actions, i.e. (sequences of words) and syntactic patterns. It reflects the input children receive in that caregivers also explain/show objects directly to their children and may show them how to use objects/perform actions in front of them (Rolf et al., 2009; Schillingmann et al., 2009).

We opted for the collection of parallel data concerning vision and body postures for human tutors. Hence, the corpus allows grounding of linguistic structures in both vision and body postures. Including body postures moreover allows the evaluation of algorithms showing manipulation skills which is of interest with respect to learning in robots.

We used stereo vision to allow computational learners to reliably track object movement and interaction using both visual and depth information. With respect to vision, four cameras with two different perspectives were used: two static external cameras as well as the robot's two internal moving cameras. The latter basically mimics the "infant" view, i.e. while the external cameras were static, the robot moved its eyes (and thus the cameras) and focused on the tutor's hand performing the actions, thus reflecting how a child may focus her/his attention to the important aspects of a scene/a performance of her/his caregiver.

3.2 Participants

A total of 27 adult human subjects participated in data collection (7 male, 20 female, mean age: 26). Subjects were paid for their participation.

3.3 Experimental setting

Human subjects performed pre-defined actions and simultaneously described their performances in front of the robot iCub (Metta et al., 2008); Fig. 1 depicts a human subject interacting with iCub. While interacting with iCub, human subjects' behavior was recorded. In particular, the following data were recorded simultaneously:

Figure 1: A human subject interacting with iCub.

- Speech/Audio (via a headset microphone)
- Vision/Video, static perspective (via two cameras, allowing for stereo vision)
- iCub-Vision/Video, iCub's (attentive) perspective (via iCub's two internal cameras, again allowing for stereo vision)
- Body postures (via a Kinect).

An experimental sketch showing the experimental setting including the positions of the human subject and iCub, as well as camera and Kinect positions, is illustrated in Fig. 2. As can be seen, the human subject was placed directly opposite to iCub. The two external cameras and the Kincet were placed slightly sloped opposite to the subject. Subjects were instructed about which actions should be performed via a computer screen which was operated by an experimentator.

In order to encourage subjects to perform the tutoring task rather naturally, i.e. just like they were interacting with a human (child), iCub provided feedback (Nagai and Rohlfing, 2009; Fischer et al., 2011). In particular, a gazing behavior was implemented to make the robot appear attentively following the tutoring.

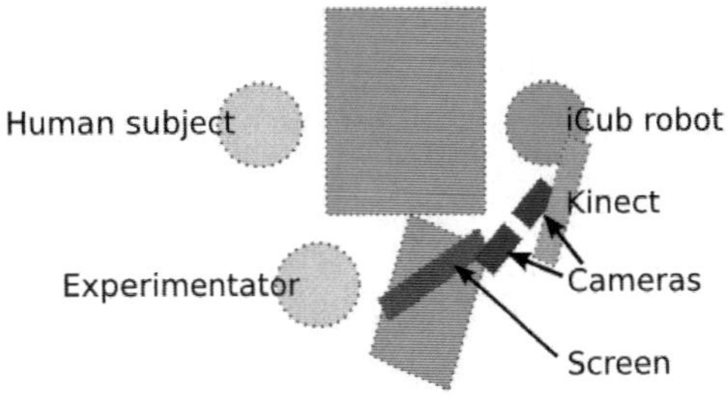

Figure 2: Experimental sketch.

3.4 Stimuli

Data were gathered in the framework of a toy cooking scenario. In particular, subjects prepared several dishes in front of iCub using toy objects. Specifically, 21 toy objects were chosen such that they were rather easy to differentiate with respect to color and/or form. The chosen objects were: pizza, pita bread, plate, bowl, spaghetti, pepper, vinegar, red pepper, lettuce leafs, tomato, onion, cucumber, cheese, toast, salami, chillies, egg, anchovy, cutting board, knife, and mushrooms. The objects are depicted in Fig. 3. Moreover, six different actions were chosen which could be executed using these objects. Again, the goal was to support rather easy identification visually (with respect to their trajectories). The chosen actions were: *showing an object*, *cutting an object (egg or tomato) into two pieces (with knife)*, *placing an object onto another one (plate, pizza, cutting board, toast)*, *putting an object into another one (bowl, pita bread)*, *pour vinegar*, and *strew pepper*. Thus, most actions were object-specific to a

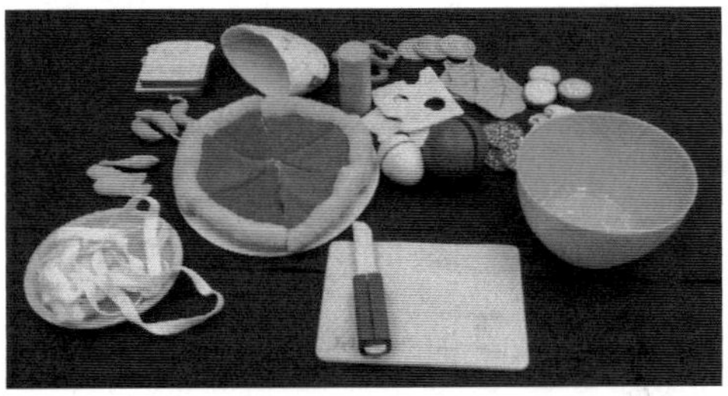

Figure 3: Utilized objects.

certain degree, i.e. they were to be executed with a certain subset of the objects each. The *show* action was to be executed using each of the objects. Furthermore, 20 different dishes, i.e. preparation processes each consisting of a sequence of actions, were created (four dishes including salad, pizza, pita bread, spaghetti and sandwich/toast, respectively). This was done in order to gather rather fluent/consistent courses of action and rather fluent communication in case of descriptions. For instance, one sequence for preparing a salad started as follows: *showing bowl, showing lettuce leafs, putting lettuce leafs into bowl, showing cutting board, showing knife, showing tomato, putting tomato onto cutting board, cutting tomato into two pieces, putting tomato pieces into bowl*, etc.

3.5 Procedure

Subjects first prepared one dish while not being recorded in order to get familiar with the task. They were instructed to perform presented actions and to describe their performance simultaneously. Moreover, they were asked to name objects and actions explicitly, since a goal of the corpus is to allow learning connections between speech, vision and body postures. Subjects were not asked to use particular words or phrases, but were free to make own choices. For instance, when being exposed to a picture of the pita bread, they were supposed to explicitly name the pita bread. Yet, they were free to choose a suitable word (or sequence of words), e.g. "Pita", "Pitatasche", "Teigtasche", "Dönertasche", "Brottasche", etc.
Actions to be performed were presented to the subjects via a computer screen; either one action was presented or – in most cases – two actions were presented at once to be executed one after another. In most cases two actions were presented in order to gain more fluent communications and courses of action. In no case more than two actions were presented together because we wanted subjects to focus on performance and not on remembering a certain course of action. Actions were presented only in the form of pictures in order to elicit rather natural language use. In particular, as mentioned previously, subjects could choose freely how to name objects and actions. An example for a screen/picture showing two actions to be performed one after another is presented in Fig. 4. An experimentator operated the screen, i.e. guided the subjects through the sequences of actions. Subjects participated for approximately one hour; only subject's actual performances were recorded, yielding approximately 20–30 minutes of usable material per subject.

Figure 4: Example screen showing the actions *show red pepper* and *put red pepper into bowl*.

3.6 Robot behavior

As mentioned previously, a gazing behavior was implemented to make the robot appear attentively following the tutoring. In particular, the robot's gaze followed a subject's presentation of an action by gazing at her/his right wrist. At times when subjects did not move their hands (to present actions) the robot was looking around, i.e. it gazed at random targets. In the following, the implementation of the robot behavior will be described in more detail.
The experimental setup shown in Fig. 2 allows the system to observe a person in front of the robot iCub. While the presentation task was performed by the person, the robot was supposed to gaze at the right wrist of this person. Via the Kinect data it was possible to acquire the body posture of the robot's interaction partner. We extracted the location of the wrist and represented the Cartesian position in the coordinate system of the robot. This position was then used as the target to generate the head and eye movements. The movement was executed by the *iKinGaze* module available in the iCub software repository (Pattacini, 2010).
Next to this "tracking" behavior of the robot we also used a "background" behavior. The "background" behavior then drew randomly new targets $\mathbf{x}_{targ}$(in meter) from the uniform distribution $\Omega \in [-1.5, -1, 5] \times [-0.2, 0.2] \times [0.2, 0, 4]$ in front of the robot. After convergence to the target the behavior waited for $t = 3$ seconds before a new target was drawn. The switch from "background" behavior to "tracking" behavior was triggered if new targets arrived from the Kinect-based tracking component. This behavior stayed active

as long as targets were received. If no targets were arriving during $t = 2$ sec. after the gazing converged on the last target, the "background" behavior took over. Due to the difference in distance between targets, the motion duration was different as well. Therefore, time delays were added to the target generation, which resulted in a more natural behavior of the robot gazing.

4 Acquired data

In order to record synchronized data from the external sensors, the robot system and the experimental control software, we utilized a dedicated framework for the acquisition of multimodal human-robot interaction data sets (Wienke et al., 2012). The framework and the underlying technology (Wienke and Wrede, 2011) allows to directly capture the network communication of robotics software components. Through this approach, system-internal data from the iCub such as its proprioception and stereo cameras images can be synchronously captured and transformed into an RETF[1]-described log-file format with explicit time and type information. Moreover, additional recording devices such as the Kinect sensors, the external pair of stereo cams or the audio input from a close-talk microphone are captured directly with this system and stored persistently. An example of the acquired parallel data is provided by Fig. 5 while Table 6 summarizes the technical aspects of the acquired data.
The applied framework also supports the automatic export and conversion of synchronized parts of the multimodal data set to common formats used by other 3rd party tools such as the annotation tool ELAN (Sloetjes and Wittenburg, 2008) used for ground truth annotation of the acquired corpus. In this experiment, we additionally captured the logical state of the experiment control software which allowed us to efficiently post-process the raw data and, e.g., automatically provide cropped video files containing only single utterances. A logical state corresponds to the image seen at the screen by a human subject at a certain time, showing the action(s) to be performed.

The acquired corpus contains in total 11.45 hours / approx. 2.3 TB of multimodal input data recorded in 27 trials. Each trial was recorded in about 1 hour of wallclock time and cropped to 20–30 minutes of effective parallel data. While in 5

[1]Robot Engineering Task-Force, cf. http://retf.info/

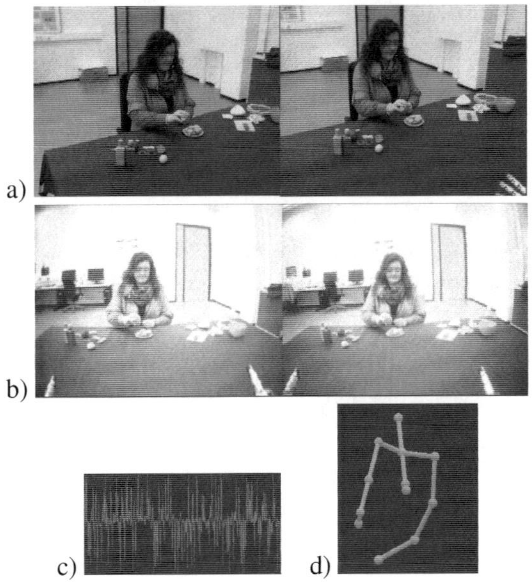

Figure 5: Example of acquired parallel data comprising a) visual data from two static cameras, b) visual data from two cameras contained in the robot's eyes, c) audio and d) body posture data recorded by the Kinect. In this example the subject is preparing a sandwich, and currently strewing pepper onto it.

cases not all of the parallel data streams are available due to difficulties with the robot and the wireless microphones, we decided to leave this data in the corpus to evaluate machine learning processes addressing learning from one or a subset of the modalities only, e.g. blind segmentation of a speech stream.
From the data logs, we exported audio (in AAC format) and the 4 synchronized video (with H.264 encoding) files (MP4 container format) for each trial with an additional ELAN project file for annotation. This annotation is currently carried out; a screenshot of acquired data and corresponding annotations in ELAN is depicted in Fig. 7. It comprises annotation of errors, as well as starting and end points for both presented actions and spoken utterances. In particular, in case of speech word transcriptions are added, while in case of vision actions are annotated in the form of predicate logic formulas. Hence, once the corpus is preprocessed, it is also suitable for the evaluation of models learning from symbolic input with respect to data from one or more domains. For instance, one could explore the acquisition of syntactic patterns from speech by providing parallel visual context

#	Device	Description	Data type	Frequency	Dimension	Throughput
1	Cam 1	Scene video	`rst.vision.Image`	≈ 30 Hz	$640 \times 480 \times 3$	≈ 28 MB/s
2	Cam 2	Scene video	`rst.vision.Image`	≈ 30 Hz	$640 \times 480 \times 3$	≈ 28 MB/s
3	Mic 1	Speech	`rst.audition.SoundChunk`	≈ 50 kHz	1-2	≈ 0.5 MB/s
4	iCub Cam 1	Ego left	`bottle/yarp::sig::Image`	≈ 30 Hz	$320 \times 240 \times 3$	≈ 7 MB/s
5	iCub Cam 2	Ego right	`bottle/yarp::sig::Image`	≈ 30 Hz	$320 \times 240 \times 3$	≈ 7 MB/s
6	Kinect	Body posture	`TrackedPosture3DFloat`[2]	≈ 30 Hz	36	≈ 6 kB/s
7	Control	Logical state	string	≈ 0.05 Hz	-	≈ 5 B/s

Figure 6: Description of acquired data streams, type specifications, average frequency, data dimension and throughput as measured during recording.

information either in sub-symbolic form or in the form of predicate logic formulas.

Figure 7: Example of acquired data and corresponding annotations in ELAN.

Word transcriptions for utterances for the whole data set are not yet available. According to the experimentators' impressions, most subjects indeed used, as desired, rather short sentences. Furthermore, a few subjects tried to vary their linguistic descriptions, i.e. to use different sentences for each description. Thus, the corpus appears to cover not only several examples of rather simple linguistic constructions with variations across speakers, but moreover input examples with a rather large degree of linguistic variation for a single speaker, hence providing examples of more challenging data.
We will make the corpus available to the public once post-processing is completely finished.

5 Conclusion

In this paper, we have described the design and acquisition of a German multimodal data set for the development and evaluation of grounded language acquisition models and algorithms enabling corresponding abilities in robots. The corpus contains parallel data including speech, visual data from four different cameras with different perspectives and body posture data from multiple speakers/actors. Among others, learning processes that may be evaluated using the corpus include: acquisition of several linguistic structures, acquisition of visual structures, concept formation, acquisition of generalized patterns which abstract over different speakers and actors, establishment of correspondences between structures from different domains and acquisition of manipulation skills.

Acknowledgments

We are deeply grateful to Jan Moringen, Michael Götting and Stefan Krüger for providing technical support. We wish to thank Luci Filinger, Christina Lehwalder, Anne Nemeth and Frederike Strunz for support in data collection and annotation. This work has been funded by the German Research Foundation DFG within the Collaborative Research Center 673 *Alignment in Communication* and the Center of Excellence *Cognitive Interaction Technology*. Andre Lemme is funded by FP7 under GA. No. 248311-AMARSi.

References

Afra Alishahi and Suzanne Stevenson. 2008. A computational model of early argument structure acquisition. *Cognitive Science*, 32(5):789–834.

Toomas Altosaar, Louis ten Bosch, Guillaume Aimetti, Christos Koniaris, Kris Demuynck, and Henk van den Heuvel. 2010. A speech corpus for modeling language acquisition: Caregiver. In *Proceed-*

ings of the International Conference on Language Resources and Evaluation.

Kristina Nilsson Björkenstam and Mats Wirn. 2013. Multimodal annotation of parent-child interaction in a free-play setting. In *Proceedings of the Thirteenth International Conference on Intelligent Virtual Agents.*

Nancy C. Chang and Tiago V. Maia. 2001. Learning grammatical constructions. In *Proceedings of the 23rd Cognitive Science Society Conference.*

Kerstin Fischer, Kilian Foth, Katharina J. Rohlfing, and Britta Wrede. 2011. Mindful tutors: Linguistic choice and action demonstration in speech to infants and to a simulated robot. *Interaction Studies*, 12(1):134–161.

Judith Gaspers and Philipp Cimiano. in press. A computational model for the item-based induction of construction networks. *Cognitive Science.*

Stevan Harnad. 1990. The symbol grounding problem. *Physica D: Nonlinear Phenomena*, 42(1-3):335–346.

Tom Kwiatkowski, Sharon Goldwater, Luke Zettlemoyer, and Mark Steedman. 2012. A probabilistic model of syntactic and semantic acquisition from child-directed utterances and their meanings. In *Proceedings of the 13th Conference of the European Chapter of the Association for Computational Linguistics.*

Brian MacWhinney. 2000. *The CHILDES Project: Tools for analyzing talk.* Mahwah, NJ.

Giorgio Metta, Giulio Sandini, David Vernon, Lorenzo Natale, and Francesco Nori. 2008. The iCub humanoid robot: an open platform for research in embodied cognition. In *Proceedings of the 8th Workshop on Performance Metrics for Intelligent Systems*, pages 50–56, New York, NY. ACM.

Yukie Nagai and Katharina J. Rohlfing. 2009. Computational analysis of motionese toward scaffolding robot action learning. *IEEE Transactions on Autonomous Mental Development*, 1:44–54.

Ugo Pattacini. 2010. *Modular Cartesian Controllers for Humanoid Robots: Design and Implementation on the iCub.* Ph.D. thesis, RBCS, Istituto Italiano di Tecnologia, Genova.

Okko Räsänen, Unto K. Laine, and Toomas Altosaar. 2009. Computational language acquisition by statistical bottom-up processing. In *Proceedings Interspeech.*

Okko Räsänen. 2011. A computational model of word segmentation from continuous speech using transitional probabilities of atomic acoustic events. *Cognition*, 120:149176.

Okko Räsänen. 2012. Computational modeling of phonetic and lexical learning in early language acquisition: existing models and future directions. *Speech Communication*, 54:975–997.

Matthias Rolf, Marc Hanheide, and Katharina J. Rohlfing. 2009. Attention via synchrony. making use of multimodal cues in social learning. *IEEE Transactions on Autonomous Mental Development*, 1:55–67.

Lars Schillingmann, Britta Wrede, and Katharina J. Rohlfing. 2009. A computational model of acoustic packaging. *IEEE Transactions on Autonomous Mental Development*, 1:226–237.

Han Sloetjes and Peter Wittenburg. 2008. Annotation by category: Elan and iso dcr. In *Proceedings of the International Conference on Language Resources and Evaluation.*

Johannes Wienke and Sebastian Wrede. 2011. A Middleware for Collaborative Research in Experimental Robotics. In *IEEE/SICE International Symposium on System Integration (SII2011)*, Kyoto, Japan. IEEE.

Johannes Wienke, David Klotz, and Sebastian Wrede. 2012. A Framework for the Acquisition of Multimodal Human-Robot Interaction Data Sets with a Whole-System Perspective. In *LREC Workshop on Multimodal Corpora for Machine Learning: How should multimodal corpora deal with the situation?*, Istanbul, Turkey.

Chen Yu, Linda B. Smith, and Alfredo F. Pereira. 2008. Grounding word learning in multimodal sensorimotor interaction. In *Proceedings of the 30th Annual Conference of the Cognitive Science Society.*

Chen Yu. 2006. Learning syntax-semantics mappings to bootstrap word learning. In *Proceedings of the 28th Annual Conference of the Cognitive Science Society (2006) Key: citeulike:5276016.*

Towards a computational model of grammaticalization and lexical diversity

Christian Bentz
University of Cambridge, DTAL
9 West Road, CB3 9DA
cb696@cam.ac.uk

Paula Buttery
University of Cambridge, DTAL
9 West Road, CB3 9DA
pjb48@cam.ac.uk

Abstract

Languages use different lexical inventories to encode information, ranging from small sets of simplex words to large sets of morphologically complex words. Grammaticalization theories argue that this variation arises as the outcome of diachronic processes whereby co-occurring words merge to one word and build up complex morphology. To model these processes we present a) a quantitative measure of lexical diversity and b) a preliminary computational model of changes in lexical diversity over several generations of merging higly frequent collocates.

1 Introduction

All languages share the property of being carriers of information. However, they vastly differ in terms of the exact encoding strategies they adopt. For example, German encodes information about number, gender, case, tense, aspect, etc. in a multitude of different articles, pronouns, nouns, adjectives and verbs. This abundant set of word forms contrasts with a smaller set of uninflected words in English.

Crucially, grammaticalization theories (Heine and Kuteva, 2007, 2002; Bybee 2006, 2003; Hopper and Traugott, 2003; Lehmann, 1985) demonstrate that complex morphological marking can derive diachronically by merging originally independent word forms that frequently co-occur. Over several generations of language learning and usage such grammaticalization and entrenchment processes can gradually increase the complexity of word forms and hence the lexical diversity of languages.

To model these processes Section 2 will present a quantitative measure of lexical diversity based on Zipf-Mandelbrots law, which is also used as a biodiversity index (Jost, 2006). Based on this measure we present a preliminary computational model to reconstruct the gradual change from lexically constrained to lexically rich languages in Section 3. We therefore use a simple grammaticalization algorithm and show how historical developments towards higher lexical diversity match the variation in lexical diversity of natural languages today. This suggests that *synchronic* variation in lexical diversity can be explained as the outcome of *diachronic* language change.

The computational model we present will therefore help to a) understand the diversity of lexical encoding strategies across languages better, and b) to further uncover the diachronic processes leading up to these synchronic differences.

2 Zipf's law as a measure of lexical diversity

Zipf-Mandelbrot's law (Mandelbrot, 1953; Zipf, 1949) states that ordering of words according to their frequencies in texts will render frequency distributions of a specific shape: in general, few words have high frequencies, followed by a middle ground of medium frequencies and a long tail of low frequency items.

However, a series of studies pointed out that there are subtle differences in frequency distributions for different texts and languages (Bentz et al., forthcoming; Ha et al., 2006; Popescu and Altmann, 2008). Namely, languages with complex morphology tend to have longer tails of low frequency words than languages with simplex morphology. The parameters of Zipf-Mandelbrot's law reflect these differences, and can be used as a quantitative measure of lexical diversity.

2.1 Method

We use the definition of ZM's law as captured by equation (1):

$$f(r_i) = \frac{C}{\beta + r_i^{\alpha}},$$
$$C > 0, \alpha > 0, \ \beta > -1, \ i = 1, 2, \ldots, n \qquad (1)$$

where $f(r_i)$ is the frequency of the word of the ith rank (r_i), n is the number of ranks, C is a normalizing factor and α and β are parameters. To illustrate this, we use parallel texts of the *Universal Declaration of Human Rights* (UDHR) for Fijian, English, German and Hungarian. For frequency distributions of these texts (with tokens delimited by white spaces) we can approximate the best fitting parameters of the ZM law by means of maximum likelihood estimation (Izsák, 2006; Murphy, 2013). In double logarithmic space (see Figure 1) the normalizing factor C would shift the line of best fit upwards or downwards, α is the slope of this line and β is Mandelbrot's (1953) corrective for the fact that the line of best fit will deviate from a straight line for higher frequencies (upper left corner in Figure 1).

As can be seen in Figure 1 Fijian has higher frequencies towards the lowest ranks (upper left corner) but the shortest tail of words with frequency one (horizontal bars in the lower right corner). For Hungarian the pattern runs the other way round: it has the lowest frequencies towards the low ranks and a long tail of words with frequency one. German and English lie between these. These patterns are reflected in ZM parameter values. Namely, Fijian has the highest parameters, followed by English, German and Hungarian. By trend there is a negative relationship between ZM parameters and lexical diversity: low lexical diversity is associated with high parameters, high diversity is associated with low parameters. Cross-linguistically this effect can be used to measure lexical diversity by means of approximating the parameters of ZM's law for parallel texts.

In the following, we will present a computational model to elicit the diachronic pathways of grammaticalization through which a

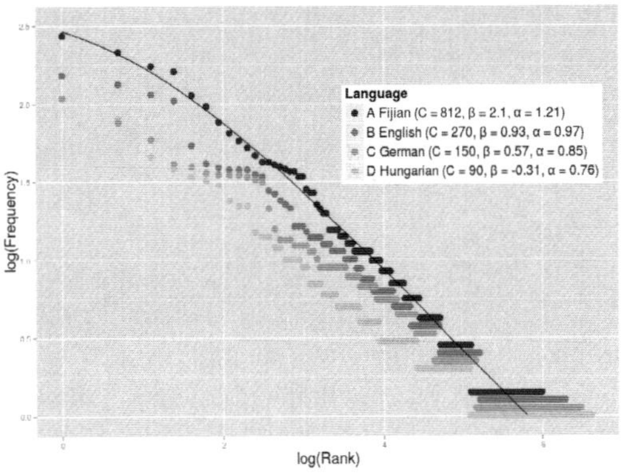

Figure 1: Zipf frequency distributions for four natural languages (Fijian, English, German, Hungarian). Plots are in log-log space, values 0.15, 0.1 and 0.05 were added to Fijian, English and German log-frequencies to avoid overplotting. Values for the Zipf-Mandelbrot parameters are given in the legend. The straight black line is the line of best fit for Fijian.

low lexical diversity language like Fijian might develop towards a high diversity language like Hungarian.

3 Modelling changes in lexical diversity

Grammaticalization theorists have long claimed that synchronic variation in word complexity and lexical diversity might be the outcome of diachronic processes. Namely, the grammaticalization cline from *content item* >*grammatical word* >*clitic* >*inflectional affix* is seen as a ubiquitous process in language change (Hopper and Traugott, 2003: 7). In the final stage frequently co-occurring words merge by means of phonological fusion (Bybee, 2003: 617) and hence 'morphologize' to built inflections and derivations.

Typical examples of a full cline of grammaticalization are the Old English noun *līc* 'body' becoming the derivational suffix *-ly*, the inflectional future in Romance languages such as Italian *canterò* 'I will sing' derived from Latin *cantare habeo* 'I have to sing', or Hungarian inflectional elative and inessive case markers derived from a noun originally meaning 'interior' (Heine and Kuteva, 2007: 66). These processes can cause languages to distinguish between a panoply of different word forms. For example, Hungarian displays up to 20 different noun forms where English would use a single form (e.g. *ship* corresponding to Hungarian *hajó* 'ship', *hajóban* 'in the ship', *hajóba* 'into the ship', etc.).

As a consequence, once the full grammaticalization cline is completed this will increase the lexical diversity of a language. Note, however, that borrowings (loanwords) and neologisms can also increase lexical diversity. Hence, a model of changes in lexical diversity will have to take both grammaticalization and new vocabulary into account.

3.1 The model

Text: We use the Fijian UDHR as our starting point for two reasons: a) Fijian is a language that is well known to be largely lacking complex morphology, b) the UDHR is a parallel text and hence allows us to compare different languages by controlling for constant information content. Fijian has relatively low lexical diversity and high ZM parameter values (see Figure 1). The question is whether we can simulate a simple merging process over several generations that will transform the frequency distribution of the original Fijian text to fit the frequency distribution of the morphologically and lexically rich Hungarian text. To answer this question, we simulate the outcome of grammaticalization on the frequency distributions in the following steps:

Simulation: Our program takes a given text of generation i, calculates a frequency distribution for this generation, changes the text along various operations given below, and gives the frequency distribution of the text for a new generation $i+1$ as output.

We take the original UDHR in Fijian as our starting point in generation 0 and run the program for consecutive generations. We simulate the change of this text over several generations of language learning and usage by varying the following variables:

- p_m: Rank bigrams according to their frequency and merge the highest p_m percent of them to one word. This simulates a simple grammaticalization process whereby two separate words that are frequent collocates are merged to one word.

- p_v: Percentage of words replaced by new words. Choose p_v of words randomly and replace all instances of these words by inverting the letters. This simulates neologisms and loanwords replacing deprecated words.

- r_R: Range of ranks to be included in p_v replacements. If set to 0, vocabulary from anywhere in the distribution will be randomly replaced.

- n_G: Number of generations to simulate.

This simulation essentially allows us to vary the degree of grammaticalization by means of varying p_m, and also to control for the fact that frequency distributions might change due to loanword borrowing and introduction of new vocabulary (p_v). Additionally, r_R allows us to vary the range of ranks where new words might replace deprecated ones. For frequency distributions calculated by generations we approximate ZM parameters by maximum likelihood estimations and therefore document the change of their shape.

Results: Figure 2 illustrates a simulation of how the low lexical diversity language Fijian approaches quantitative lexical properties similar to the Hungarian text just by means of merging high-frequent collocates. While the frequency distribution of Fijian in generation 0 still reflects the original ZM values, the ZM parameter values after 6 generations of grammaticalization have become much closer to the values of the Hungarian UDHR:

Fij ($n_G = 0$): $\alpha = 1.21, \beta = 2.1, C = 812$
Fij ($n_G = 6$): $\alpha = 0.70, \beta = -0.22, C = 73$
Hun ($n_G = 0$): $\alpha = 0.76, \beta = -0.31, C = 90$

Note, that in this model there is actually no replacement of vocabulary necessary to arrive at frequency distributions that correspond to high lexical diversity variants. After only six generations of merging 2.5% of bigrams to a single grammaticalized word the Fijian UDHR has ZM parameter properties very close to the Hungarian UDHR. However, in future research we want to scrutinize the effect of parameter changes on frequency distributions in more depth and in accordance

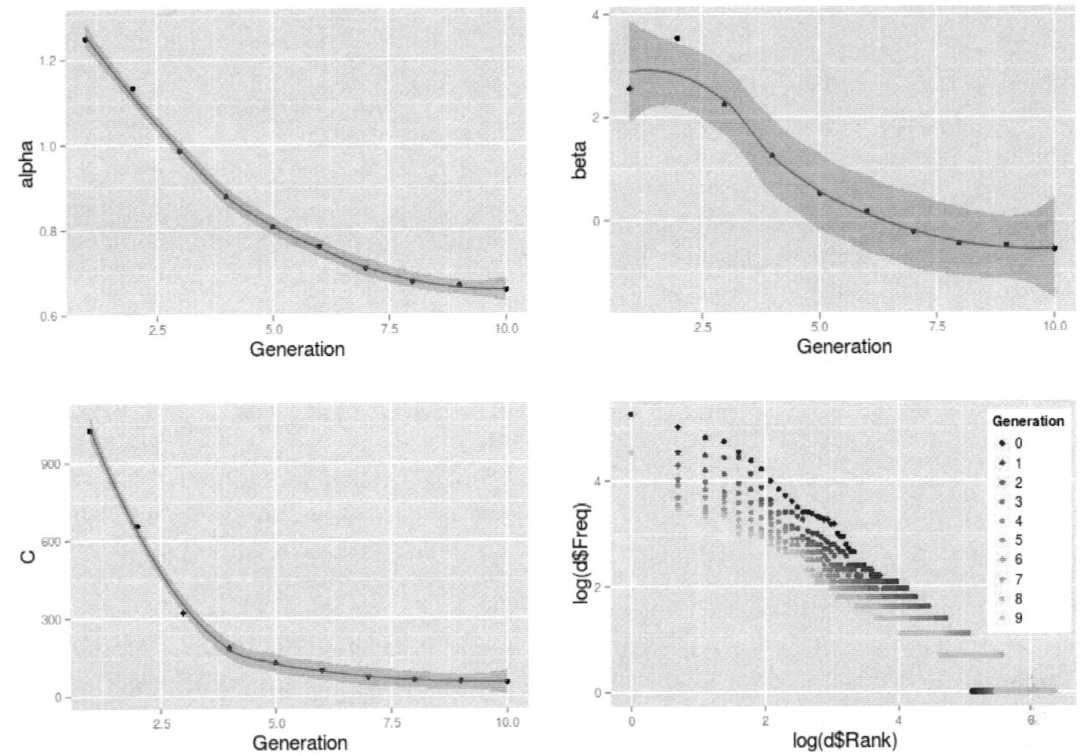

Figure 2: Simulation of grammaticalization processes and their reflections in Zipf distributions for variable values $p_m = 2.5$, $p_v = 0, r_R = 0, n_G = 10$. Changes of α are shown in the upper left panel, changes in β are shown in the upper right panel, changes in C are shown in the lower left panel, and changes in log-transformed frequency distributions are illustrated in the lower right panel.

with estimations derived from historical linguistic studies.

4 Discussion

We have pointed out in Section 2 that lexical diversity can be measured cross-linguistically by means of calculating frequency distributions for parallel texts and approximating the corresponding ZM parameters in a maximum likelihood estimation.

It is assumed that cross-linguistic variation is the outcome of diachronic processes of grammaticalization, whereby highly frequent bigrams are merged into a single word. The preliminary computational model in Section 3 showed that indeed even by a strongly simplified grammaticalization process a text with low lexical diversity (Fijian UDHR) can gain lexical richness over several generations, and finally match the quantitative properties of a lexically rich language (Hungarian UDHR).

However, there are several caveats that need to be addressed in future research:

- More models with varying parameters need to be run to scrutinize the interaction between new vocabulary (loanwords, neologisms) and grammaticalization.
- The grammaticalization algorithm used is overly simplified. A more realistic picture is possible by using POS tagged and parsed texts to ensure that only certain parts of speech in certain syntactic contexts grammaticalize (e.g. pre- and postpositions in combination with nouns).
- The model could be elaborated by considering not only bigram frequencies but also frequencies of the individual words and more complex frequency measures (see Schmid, 2010).

5 Conclusion

Languages display an astonishing diversity when it comes to lexical encoding of information. This *synchronic* variation in encoding strategies is most likely the outcome of *diachronic* processes of language change. We have argued that lexical diversity can be measured quantitatively with reference to the parameters of Zipf-Mandelbrot's law, and that pathways of change in lexical diversity can be modelled computationally. Elaboration and refinement of these models will help to better understand linguistic diversity as the outcome of processes on historical and evolutionary time scales.

References

Marco Baroni. 2009. Distributions in text. In Anke Lüdeling and Merja Kytö (eds.), *Corpus Linguistics. An international handbook*. Berlin/ New York, Mouton de Gruyter, pages 803-826.

Christian Bentz, Douwe Kiela, Felix Hill, and Paula Buttery. forthcoming. Zipf's law and the grammar of languages. In *Corpus Linguistics and Linguistic Theory*.

Joan Bybee. 2006. From usage to grammar: The mind's repsonse to repetition. In *Language*, volume 82 (4), pages 711-733.

Joan Bybee. 2003. Mechanisms of change in grammaticization: the role of frequency. In B. D. Joseph and J. Janda(eds.), *The Handbook of Historical Linguistics*. Oxford, Blackwell, pages 711-733.

Le Q. Ha, Darryl Stewart, Philip Hanna, and F. Smith. 2006. Zipf and type-token rules for the English, Spanish, Irish and Latin languages. In *Web Journal of Formal, Computational and Cognitive Linguistics*, volume 8.

Bernd Heine and Tania Kuteva. 2007. *The Genesis of Grammar: A Reconstruction*. Oxford University Press.

Bernd Heine and Tania Kuteva. 2002. *World lexicon of grammaticalization*. Cambridge University Press.

Paul J. Hopper and Elizabeth C. Traugott. 2003. *Grammaticalization*. Cambridge University Press.

János Izsák. 2006. Some practical aspects of fitting and testing the Zipf-Mandelbrot model: A short essay. In *Scientometrics*, volume 67(1), pages 107-120.

Lou Jost. 2006. Entropy and diversity. In *OIKOS*, volume 113(2), pages 363-375.

Christian Lehmann. 1985. Grammaticalization: Synchronic variation and diachronic change. In *Lingua e stile*, volume 20, pages 303-318.

Benoit Mandelbrot. 1953. An informational theory of the statistical structure of language. In William Jackson (ed.), *Communication Theory*. Butterworths Scientific Publications, London, pages 468-502.

Laura Murphy. 2013. *R package likelihood: Methods for maximum likelihood estimation*. Retrieved from cran.r-project.org/web/packages/likelihood

Ioan-Iovitz Popescu, and Gabriel Altmann. 2008. Hapax legomena and language typology. In *Journal of Quantitative Linguistics*, volume 15(4), pages 370378.

Hans-J. Schmid. 2010. Does frequency in text instantiate entrenchment in the cognitive system? In Dylan Glynn and Kerstin Fischer (eds.), *Quantitative methods in cognitive semantics: Corpus-driven approaches*. Berlin, Walter de Gruyter, pages 101-133.

George K. Zipf. 1949. *Human behavior and the principle of least effort*. Addison, Cambridge (Massachusetts).

How Well Can a Corpus-Derived Co-Occurrence Network Simulate Human Associative Behavior?

Gemma Bel Enguix Reinhard Rapp Michael Zock

Aix-Marseille Université, Laboratoire d'Informatique Fondamentale
UMR 7279, Case 901, 163 Avenue de Luminy, F-13288 Marseille

gemma.belenguix@gmail.com reinhardrapp@gmx.de zock@free.fr

Abstract

Free word associations are the words people spontaneously come up with in response to a stimulus word. Such information has been collected from test persons and stored in databases. A well known example is the Edinburgh Associative Thesaurus (EAT). We will show in this paper that this kind of knowledge can be acquired automatically from corpora, enabling the computer to produce similar associative responses as people do. While in the past test sets typically consisted of approximately 100 words, we will use here a large part of the EAT which, in total, comprises 8400 words. Apart from extending the test set, we consider different properties of words: saliency, frequency and part-of-speech. For each feature categorize our test set, and we compare the simulation results to those based on the EAT. It turns out that there are surprising similarities which supports our claim that a corpus-derived co-occurrence network can simulate human associative behavior, i.e. an important part of language acquisition and verbal behavior.

1 Introduction

Word associations in general and free word association in particular (Galton, 1879) have been used by psychologists of various schools[1] to understand the human mind (memory, cognition, language) and the hidden mechanisms driving peoples' thoughts, utterances, and actions. In the case of free word associations, a person typically hears or reads a word, and is asked to produce the first other word coming to mind. Kent & Rosanoff (1910) have used this method for comparisons, introducing to this end 100 emotionally neutral test words. Having conducted the first large scale study of word associations (1000 test persons) they reached the conclusion that there was a great uniformity concerning people's associations, that is, speakers of a language share stable, comparable associative networks (Istifci, 2010).

In this paper, we are mainly interested in the automatic acquisition of associations by computer. More precisely, we want to check whether a corpus-based method allows us to build automatically an associative network akin to the one in peoples' mind, that is, a network able to mimic human behavior. This means, given a stimulus word the system is supposed to produce the same responses as people do. We know since the old Greeks that thoughts and their expressions (words) are linked via associations. Yet, what we still do not know is the nature of these links. Also, links vary in terms of strength. Associationist learning theory (Schwartz & Reisberg, 1991) explains how these strengths (or weights) are acquired. The strength between two perceived events increases by a constant fraction of a maximally possible increment at each co-occurrence, and decreases in the opposite case.

Wettler et al. (2005) have shown that this mechanism can be replicated by looking at word co-occurrence frequencies in large text collections. But there had been earlier corpus-linguistic work: For example, Wettler & Rapp (1989) compared several association measures in order to find search terms to be used for queries in information retrieval. Church & Hanks (1990) suggested to use *mutual information*, an information theoretic measure, for computing association strength. Prior to this, a lot of work had been done without reliance of corpora. For example, Collins & Loftus (1975) used associative semantic networks to show the distance between words. Others (Rosenzweig, 1961:358; Ekpo-Ufot, 1978) tried to show the universal status of a large subset of associations. While all these findings are important, we will not consider them further

[1] For example, *cognitive psychology* (Collins and Loftus, 1975,), *psycholinguistics* (Clark, 1970) and *psychoanalysis* (Freud, 1901; Jung & Riklin, 1906).

here. Rather we will focus on the claim that a - corpus-derived co-occurrence network is able to mimic human associative behavior.

Such a network consists of nodes, which in our case correspond to words (or lemmas), and of weights connecting the nodes. The strengths of these weights are computed on the basis of word co-occurrence data, and by optionally applying an association measure. But there are many association measures. Given their number and diversity some researchers (Evert & Krenn, 2001) felt that there was a need to define some criteria and methods in order to allow for quantitative comparisons via task-based evaluations. Pursuing a similar goal, Pecina & Schlesinger (2006) compared 82 different association measures for collocation extraction, while Hoang et al. (2009) classified them. Michelbacher et al. (2011) investigated the potential of asymmetric association measures, i.e. "associations whose associational strength is significantly greater in one direction (e.g., from *Pyrrhic* to *victory*) than in the other (e.g., from *victory* to *Pyrrhic*)". Washtell & Markert (2009) tried to determine whether word associations should be computed via window-based co-occurrence counts or rather via a windowless approach measuring the distances between words.

Our work is related to previous studies comparing human word associations with those derived from corpus statistics (e.g. Wettler et al., 2005; Tamir, 2005, Seidensticker, 2006). The main differences are that we categorize our stimulus words and present results for each class, and that we have a stronger focus on the graph aspect of our network.

2 Resources and processing

In order to simulate human associative behavior via corpora, we need them to encode knowledge that people typically have, that is, encyclopedic or universally shared knowledge (e.g. Paris capital of France) and episodic knowledge (i.e. knowledge momentarily true: Nadal winner of the French Open). To meet these goals we decided to use the *British National Corpus* (BNC, Burnard & Aston, 1998) as it is well balanced and relatively large (about 100 million words of contemporary British English).

To lemmatize the corpus we used the NLTK (Bird et al., 2009) which for this purpose utilizes information from WordNet. Hence, inflected forms (e.g. *wheels* or *bigger*) were replaced by their base forms (e.g. *wheel* or *big*). This reduces noise and data sparsity while improving speed and accuracy during evaluation. Since this latter is based on exact string matching, our system would consider *wheels*, produced in response to *car*, as a mistake as the primary associative response of the test persons is *wheel*, the singular form. Lemmatization solves this problem. Since we were interested here only in content words (nouns, verbs, and adjectives) we removed all other words from the BNC.

To evaluate the performance of our system we compared its results with the associations collected by Kiss et al. (1973), the *Edinburgh Associative Thesaurus*. The association norms of the EAT were produced by presenting each stimulus word to 100 subjects, and by collecting their responses. The subjects were 17 to 22 year old British students. Table 1 shows the associations produced by at least five participants in response to the stimulus words *bath* and *cold* together with the number of participants producing them.

bath		*cold*	
observed response	number of subjects	observed response	number of subjects
water	20	hot	34
tub	8	ice	10
clean	5	warm	7
hot	5	water	5

Table 1: Extracts from the EAT for the stimulus words *bath* and *cold*.

The EAT lists the associations to 8400 stimulus words. Since we were only interested in nouns, verbs, and adjectives, we eliminated all other words and also multiword units (e.g. *a lot*). After having lemmatized the data with the NLTK we obtained a list of 5910 test items which is considerably more than the usual 100 used in many previous studies (e.g. Wettler et al., 2005).

3 A graph-based approach for computing word associations

Unlike previous work (Wettler et al. 2005; Church & Hanks, 1990) which is described in the terminology of the well known vector space model, in the construction of the current system we had a graph-based approach in mind so we describe the system in such terms. We built up a graph on the basis of the nouns, verbs, and adjectives occurring in the corpus, these tokens being the nodes of the graph.[2] The links (also called

[2] As preliminary experiments have shown, including function words in the graph can create noise in the retrieval of

weights, connections, or edges) between these nodes are zero at the beginning, and are incremented by one whenever the two connected words co-occur in the corpus as direct neighbors.[3] Put differently, the weight of each link represents the number of times two words (nodes) co-occur in the corpus.

The associations to a given stimulus word are calculated by searching the nodes which are direct neighbors of this stimulus word, and by ranking them according to the weights of the connections. Given a graph G=V,E with V={i,j,...,n} as its set of vertices and E as its set of edges linking pairs of nodes over V, we express by N(i) the neighborhood of a node i $\in$V, where N(i) is defined as every j$\in$V | $e_{i,j}$ $\in$E.

4 Results

Given the way this network is built, one could expect the system to retrieve only syntagmatically related words, i.e. words often occurring in close proximity (e.g. *blue* → *sky*). Yet, to our surprise, the system also retrieves many paradigmatic associations, that is, words which can substitute each other (e.g. *blue* → *red*).

Table 2 shows some results. While not all computed primary responses are identical to the ones produced by humans (in the EAT), the responses seem perfectly plausible. This raises the question whether the answers are within the bandwidth of variation of human associative behavior.

We measured the quality of our results by counting (for all 5910 items) the number of times the subjects participating in the creation of the EAT had given the same answer as our system. This number is 6.2 on average. In comparison, the number of other subjects giving the same answer as an average test person is 5.8. If the two numbers were identical, our system would be perfectly within the range of variation of the human associative responses, i.e. our system's answers could hardly be distinguished from the ones given by a human. This is actually the case. The answers of our system are, on average, even slightly closer to the ones given by the test persons than the answers of a randomly selected test person.

associations. Hence we preferred to keep only these three categories.

[3] Note that this refers to the pre-processed corpus where all stopwords have been removed.

Stimulus Word	Human Primary Response	Computed Primary Response
afraid	fear	person
anger	hate	frustration
baby	boy	mother
bath	water	shower
beautiful	ugly	woman
bed	sleep	hospital
bible	book	God
bitter	sweet	taste
black	white	white
blossom	flower	white

Table 2: Comparison between human and computed associations for the 10 alphabetically first words of the Kent/Rosanoff (1910) list.

In the following subsections we split our set of 5910 test items into three categories to check how well each one of them matches our intuition that a corpus-derived co-occurrence network can indeed simulate human associative behavior.

4.1 Word saliency

Our goal is twofold: find out to what extend the saliency of a stimulus word has an effect on the homogeneity of human responses, and whether these findings can also be replicated in our computer simulation.

To this end we divided our 5910 EAT stimulus words into six categories, i.e. saliency classes (SC). *Saliency* is defined here as the proportion of subjects producing the *Primary Associative Response* (PAR), this latter being the response produced by the largest number of subjects.

SC 1: less than 10% producing the PAR (10.7%)
SC 2: 10 to 20% producing the PAR (36.0%)
SC 3: 20 to 30% producing the PAR (24.3%)
SC 4: 30 to 40% producing the PAR (13.3%)
SC 5: 40 to 50% producing the PAR (8.0%)
SC 6: more than 50% producing the PAR (7.6%)

The percentages at the end of each line denote the proportion of words belonging to the respective saliency class. All classes are reasonably well covered. Here are some representative words for each class:

SC 1: leader, professor, yellow
SC 2: horse, mountain, semaphore
SC 3: chief, jungle, kiss
SC 4: driver, monarchy, tornado
SC 5: aid, cell, gasoline
SC 6: black, aunt, woman

As can be seen from these examples, our intuitions do not easily allow us to make predictions concerning the saliency classifications of words.

Figure 1 (blue curve) shows how well our system performs for each class. For the words in each class we counted the average number of times a human subject had come up with the same associative response as the system. It appears that the system's performance is best for very salient words, performing less well in the opposite case. Note that this correlates perfectly well with the observed human associative behavior: Our system tends to produce the same answers as people for stimulus words yielding homogeneous human responses. Likewise, the system's answers tend to differ in cases where peoples' answers are heterogeneous.

The red curve in Figure 1 shows for each saliency class the number of persons giving the same associative answer as an average test person. As can be seen this line is almost identical to the one representing the system's performance, which means that the system's behavior is very similar to human behavior with respect to saliency.

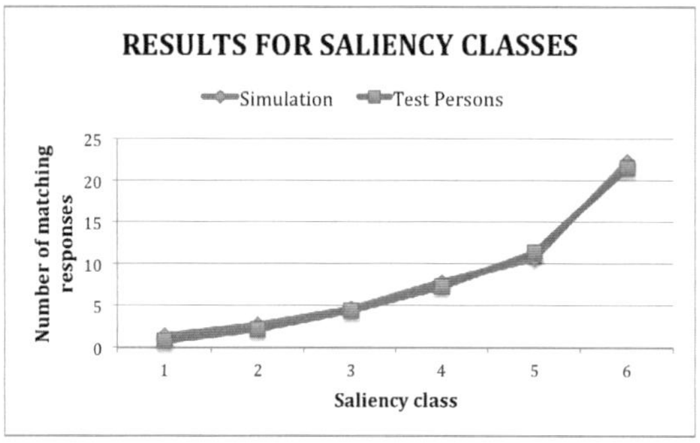

Fig. 1: Quality of our system's (blue curve) and an average test person's (red curve) performance (measured as the number of matching responses found in the EAT) with respect to saliency.

4.2 Word frequency

Encouraged by the findings for saliency, we conducted a similar experiment for word frequency. In this case the EAT stimulus words were split into frequency classes according to their corpus frequencies in the BNC.

Since a logarithmic scale seems to be appropriate for word frequencies (Rapp, 2005; van Heuven et al., in press), we used the following six frequency classes (FC):

FC1: 1 occurrence BNC (0.5%)
FC2: from 1 to 10 occurrences BNC (9.2%)
FC3: form 10 to 100 occurrences BNC (30.2%)
FC4: from 100 to 1000 occurrences BNC (42.6%)
FC5: from 1000 to 10000 occurrences BNC (17.3%)
FC6: from 10000 to 100000 occurrences BNC (0.1%)

As can be seen from the percentages at the end of each line, extremes, i.e. very high and very low frequencies are covered only marginally.

In the first group we find words like *cornucopia*, *jewelry*[4] and *quaff*, each appearing only once in the corpus, while the frequency class 6 contains only high frequency words such as the (auxiliary) verbs *be*, *do*, *have*, and *make*.

The results obtained for the frequency classes are shown in Figure 2. As can be seen, the general tendency is that the results improve with decreasing frequency. Our explanation for this is that frequent words tend to be more polysemous, and that increased ambiguity tends to yield more heterogeneous responses. For example, the ambiguous stimulus word *palm* is likely to evoke not only responses related to its *tree* sense, but also to its *hand* sense.

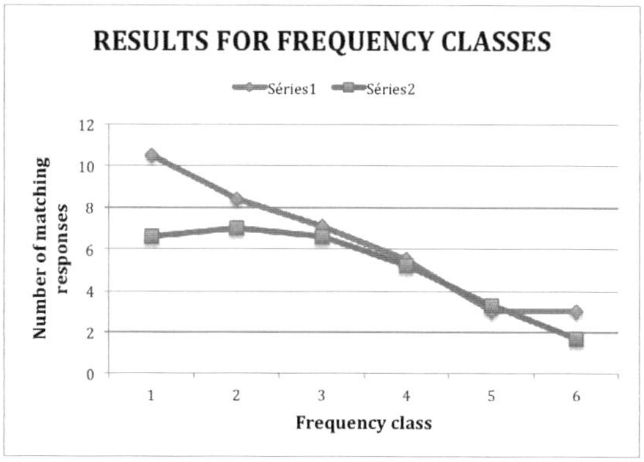

Fig. 2: Quality of our system's (blue curve) and an average test person's (red curve) performance with respect to frequency.

Whereas for mid frequency words the results for the test persons and in the simulation show a high agreement, this is not the case for high frequency and for low frequency words. For high frequency words (FC 6) a plausible explanation might be the sampling error due to the low sample size of only 0.1% of the stimulus words in the EAT test set. However, for low frequency words the sample sizes are larger and the discrepancy is clearly systematic. Our explanation is that in this case we might have a systematic sampling error concerning the observed frequencies. The simulation has an advantage because the frequency classes were set up according to

[4] Note that this is the American spelling which is rare in the BNC. The British spelling is *jewellery*.

the BNC frequencies rather than according to the subjective frequencies (= word familiarities) of the test persons. For example, the words of FC 1 are guaranteed to occur in the BNC, while it is not certain at all that the test persons ever encountered them. This leads to a systematic bias in favor of the simulation results.

4.3 Part of speech

In a last experiment we considered the results for the three parts of speech used in our system, namely nouns, verbs, and adjectives. We assigned to each word in the EAT test set its part of speech. Syntactically ambiguous words (which can belong to several parts of speech) were assigned to their most frequently occurring part of speech. Of the 5910 EAT items, 89.2% were classified as nouns, 2.4% as verbs, and 8.4% as adjectives.

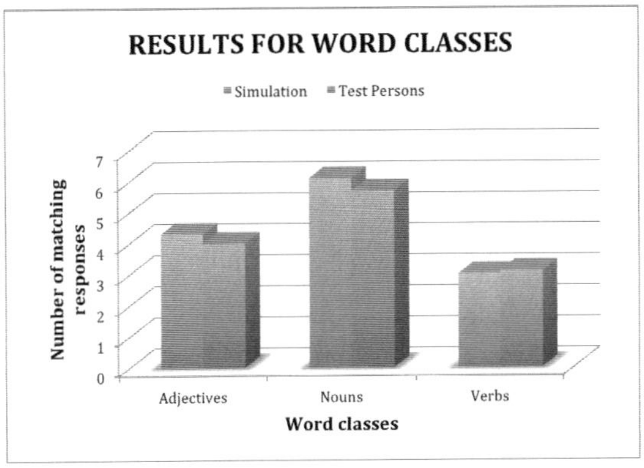

Fig. 3: Quality of our system's (blue curve) and an average test person's (red curve) performance with respect to parts of the speech.

For the three categories we obtained the results shown in Figure 3. The results are best for nouns and worst for verbs. Our explanation for this is once again average word ambiguity which is higher for verbs than it is for nouns. As with the saliency classes, we have again a high correlation between the results produced by humans and the ones produced by machine.

5 Discussion and conclusion

We have presented a novel graph-based algorithm for the computation of word associations. The goal was to check whether and to what extent an automatically built association network based on a large text corpus would yield similar results to the ones produced by humans. The results were evaluated with a test set comprising all nouns, verbs, and adjectives of the EAT stimulus words. This test set is considerably larger than the ones used in most previous computational association studies.

Contrary to what could be expected our system predicts not only syntagmatic but also paradigmatic relations. For instance, the pairs *black* → *white*, *bread* → *butter* and *boy* → *girl* are correctly computed. This shows that texts contain not only word pairs encoding syntagmatic relations but also pairs encoding paradigmatic relations. The results also show that statistical co-occurrence-based methods are suitable for tasks that traditionally were supposed to require more sophisticated symbolic approaches.

In sum, our approach allows not only to correctly predict thousands of associations, it also matches human performance in other respects: For the first time it was shown that the predictions for salient words are much better than for non-salient ones. Similarly, concerning word frequency and part of speech the simulated results also closely mimic the behavior as found in the human data.

Altogether, our results provide evidence that human associative behavior as observed in the classical association experiments can be modeled by exploiting the co-occurrences of words in large text corpora. There seems to be a circularity: (a) the word co-occurrences found in text and speech[5] appear to be externalized forms of the associations stored in the human brain, and (b) the associations stored in the brain appear to be internalized forms of the co-occurrences as found in text and speech. This contradiction disappears as soon as we realize that time has elapsed between these two events. Hence, one network may be fed by the other, and this may go on.

Note that our corpus-based approach has further virtues: (a) it allows to generate associations from corpora covering particular time spans; (b) it can produce associations based on corpora covering specific topics; (c) it accounts for the fact that languages, hence associations, change over time. Think of the ideas associated with Dominique Strauss-Kahn, one of the top candidates before the last presidential campaign in France. While the associations prior to May 18, 2011 were probably IMF, politics or election, the ones after the Sofitel event were probably quite different, shifting towards a much more delicate topic.

[5] Note that the BNC also contains transcribed speech.

Acknowledgments

This research was supported by the Marie Curie Intra European Fellowships DynNetLAc and AutoWordNet within the 7th European Community Framework Programme.

References

Bird, S.; Klein, E. and Loper, E. (2009). *Natural Language Processing with Python*. O'Reilley Media.

Burnard, L. and Aston, G. (1998). *The BNC Handbook: Exploring the British National Corpus*. Edinburgh: Edinburgh University Press.

Church, K.W. and Hanks, P. (1990). Word association norms, mutual information, and lexicography. *Computational Linguistics* 16 (1), 22–29.

Clark, H. H. (1970). Word associations and linguistic theory. In J. Lyons (Ed.), New horizons in linguistics (pp. 271-286). Baltimore: Penguin.

Collins, A. M. and Loftus, E. F. (1975). A spreading-activation theory of semantic processing. *Psychological Review* 8. Vol. 82, No. 6, 407-428.

Ekpo-Ufot, A. (1978). Word associations: a comparative study among college students in Nigeria and the United States. *Journal of Cross-Cultural Psychology*, Vol. 9(4), 455-468.

Evert, S. and Krenn, B. (2001). Methods for qualitative evaluation of lexical association measures. In *Proceedings of the 39th Annual Meeting of the Association of Computational Linguistics,* Toulouse, France, 188-915.

Freud, S. (1901/1975). The psychopathology of everyday life. Harmondsworth: Penguin. http://psychclassics.yorku.ca/Freud/Psycho/chap5.htm

Galton, F. (1879). Psychometric experiments. *Brain (2)*, 149-162.

Van Heuven, W.J.B., Mandera, P., Keuleers, E., & Brysbaert, M. (in press). Subtlex-UK: A new and improved word frequency database for British English. *Quarterly Journal of Experimental Psychology*.

Hoang, H.H, Kim, S. N. and Kan, M.Y. (2009). A re-examination of lexical association measures. *Proceedings of the Workshop on Multiword Expressions*, ACL-IJCNLP 2009, Suntec, Singapore, 31-39.

Istifci, I. (2010). Playing with words: a study on word association responses. *The Journal of International Social Research,* 3(10), 360–368

Jung, C. and F. Riklin. 1906. Experimentelle Untersuchungen über Assoziationen Gesunder. In Jung, C. G., editor, Diagnostische Assoziationsstudien, 7–145. Barth, Leipzig.

Kent, G.H. and Rosanoff, A.J. (1910). A study of association in insanity. *American Journal of Insanity*, 67, 37–96, 317–390.

Kiss, G.R., Armstrong, C., Milroy, R., and Piper, J. (1973). An associative thesaurus of English and its computer analysis. In: A. Aitken, R. Beiley, N. Hamilton-Smith (eds.): *The Computer and Literary Studies*. Edinburgh University Press.

Michelbacher, L., Evert, S. and Schütze, H. (2011). Asymmetry in corpus-derived and human associations. Corpus Linguistics and Linguistic Theory, Vo. 7, No. 2, 245–276.

Pecina, P., and Schlesinger, P. (2006). Combining association measures for collocation extraction. *Proceedings of the 21th International Conference on Computational Linguistics and 44th Annual Meeting of the Association for Computational Linguistics (COLING/ACL 2006)*, Sydney, Australia, 651-658.

Rapp, R. (2005). On the relationship between word frequency and word familiarity. In: B. Fisseni; H.-C. Schmitz; B. Schröder; P. Wagner (Hg.): *Sprachtechnologie, mobile Kommunikation und linguistische Ressourcen. Beiträge zur GLDV-Tagung 2005 in Bonn.* Frankfurt: Peter Lang. 249–263.

Rosenzweig, M. R. (1961). Comparisons among word-assocation responses in English, French, German, and Italian. *The American Journal of Psychology*, Vol. 74, No. 3, 347-360.

Schwartz, B. and Reisberg, D. (1991). *Learning and Memory*. New York: Norton.

Seidensticker, P. (2006). *Simulation von Wortassoziationen mit Hilfe von mathematischen Lernmodellen in der Psychologie*. Dissertation an der Universität Paderborn.

Tamir, R. (2005). A Random Walk through Human Associations. *Proceedings of ICDM 2005*: 442-449.

Washtell, J.; Markert, K. (2009). A comparison of windowless and window-based computational association measures as predictors of syntagmatic human associations. *Proceedings of the 2009 Conference on Empirical Methods in Natural Language Processing (EMNLP '09)*, Volume 2, 628-637

Wettler, M. and Rapp, R. (1989). A connectionist system to simulate lexical decisions in information retrieval. In: R. Pfeifer, Z. Schreter, F. Fogelman, L. Steels (eds.): *Connectionism in Perspective*. Amsterdam: Elsevier, 463–469.

Wettler, M., Rapp, R. and Sedlmeier, P. (2005). Free word associations correspond to contiguities between words in texts. *Journal of Quantitative Linguistics* 12(2), 111–122.

Agent-based modeling of language evolution

Torvald Lekvam **Björn Gambäck** **Lars Bungum**
Department of Computer and Information Science, Sem Sælands vei 7–9
Norwegian University of Science and Technology, 7491 Trondheim, Norway
torvald@lekvam.no {gamback,larsbun}@idi.ntnu.no

Abstract

Agent-based models of language evolution have received a lot of attention in the last two decades. Researchers wish to understand the origin of language, and aim to compensate for the lacking empirical evidence by utilizing methods from computer science and artificial life. The paper looks at the main theories of language evolution: biological evolution, learning, and cultural evolution. In particular, the Baldwin effect in a naming game model is elaborated on by describing a set of experimental simulations. This is on-going work and ideas for further investigating the social aspects of language evolution are also discussed.

1 Introduction

What is language? It is interesting how we can take a train of thought and transfer this into another person's mind by pushing the air around us. Human language, this complex medium that distinctly separates humans from animals, has baffled scientists for centuries. While animals also use language, even with a degree of syntax (Kako, 1999), spoken human language exhibits a vastly more complex structure and spacious variation.

To understand how language works — how it is used, its origin and fundamentals — our best information sources are the languages alive (and some extinct but documented ones). Depending on definition, there are 6,000–8,000 languages worldwide today, showing extensive diversity of syntax, semantics, phonetics and morphology (Evans and Levinson, 2009). Still, these represent perhaps only 2% of all languages that have ever existed (Pagel, 2000). As this is a rather small window, we want to look back in time. But there is a problem in linguistic history: our reconstruction techniques can only take us back some 6,000 to 7,000 years. Beyond this point, researchers can only speculate on when and how human language evolved: either as a slowly proceeding process starting millions of years (Ma) ago, e.g., 7 Ma ago with the first appearance of cognitive capacity or 2.5 Ma ago with the first manufacture of stone implements; or through some radical change taking place about 100 ka ago with the appearance of the modern humans or 50–60 ka ago when they started leaving Africa (Klein, 2008; Tattersall, 2010).

The rest of this introduction covers some key aspects of language evolution. Section 2 then focuses on computational models within the field, while Section 3 describes a specific naming game model. Finally, Section 4 discusses the results and some ideas for future work.

1.1 Theories of origin: the biological aspect

There are two main ideas in biological evolution as to why humans developed the capacity to communicate through speech. The first states that language (or more precisely the ability to bear the full structure of language) came as an *epiphenomenon*, a by-product (spandrel) of an unrelated mutation. This theory assumes that a mental language faculty could not by itself evolve by natural selection; there would simply be too many costly adaptations for it to be possible. Thus there should exist an innate capacity in the form of a *universal grammar* (Chomsky, 1986), which can hold a finite number of rules enabling us to carry any kind of language.

According to the second idea, language emerged in a strictly adaptational process (Pinker and Bloom, 1990). That is, that language evolution can be explained by natural selection, in the same way as the evolution of other complex traits like echolocation in bats or stereopsis in monkeys. Both ideas — innate capacity vs natural selection — have supporters, as well as standpoints that hold both aspects as important, but at different levels (Deacon, 2010; Christiansen and Kirby, 2003).

1.2 Theories of origin: the cultural aspect

Biology aside, the forces behind the emergence of human language are not strictly genetic (and do not operate only on a phylogenetic time scale). Kirby (2002) argues that, in addition to biological evolution, there are two more complex adaptive (dynamical) systems influencing natural language; namely *cultural evolution* (on the glossogenetic time scale) and *learning* (which operates on a individual level, on the ontogenetic time scale).

In addition, there is the interesting Darwinian idea that cultural learning can guide biological evolution, a process known as *the Baldwin effect* (Baldwin, 1896; Simpson, 1953). This theory argues that culturally learned traits (e.g., a universal understanding of grammar or a defense mechanism against a predator) can assimilate into the genetic makeup of a species. Teaching each member in a population the same thing over and over again comes with great cost (time, faulty learning, genetic complexity), and the overall population saves a lot of energy if a learned trait would become innate. On the other hand, there is a cost of genetic assimilation as it can prohibit plasticity in future generations and make individuals less adaptive to unstable environments.

There has been much debate recently whether language is a result of the Baldwin effect or not (Evans and Levinson, 2009; Chater et al., 2009; Baronchelli et al., 2012, e.g.), but questions, hypotheses, and simulations fly in both directions.

2 Language evolution and computation

Since the 90s, there has been much work on simulation of language evolution in bottom-up systems with populations of autonomous agents. The field is highly influenced by the work of Steels and Kirby, respectively, and has been summarized and reviewed both by themselves and others (Steels, 2011; Kirby, 2002; Gong and Shuai, 2013, e.g.).

Computational research in this field is limited to modeling very simplified features of human language in isolation, such as strategies for naming colors (Bleys and Steels, 2011; Puglisi et al., 2008), different aspects of morphology (Dale and Lupyan, 2012), and similar. This simplicity is important to keep in mind, since it is conceivable that certain features of language can be highly influenced by other features in real life.

A language game simulation (Steels, 1995) is a model where artificial agents interact with each other in turn in order to reach a cooperative goal; to make up a shared language of some sort, all while minimizing their cognitive effort. All agents are to some degree given the cognitive ability to bear language, but not given any prior knowledge of how language should look like or how consensus should unfold. No centralized anchors are involved: a simulation is all self-organized.

Agents are chosen (mostly at random) as hearer and speaker, and made to exchange an utterance about a certain arbitrary concept or meaning in their environment. If the agents use the same language (i.e., the utterance is understood by both parties), the conversation is a success. If the speaker utters something unfamiliar to the hearer, the conversation is termed a failure. If an agent wants to express some concept without having any utterances for it, the agent is assumed to have the ability to make one up and add this to its memory. While interpretation in real life is a complex affair, it is mostly assumed that there is a fairly direct connection between utterance and actual meaning in language game models (emotions and social situations do not bias how language is interpreted).

A simple language game normally is characterized by many synonyms spawning among the agents. As agents commence spreading their own utterances around, high-weighted words start to be preferred. Consensus is reached when all agents know the highest weighted word for each concept. Commonly, the agents aim to reach a single coherent language, but the emergence of multilingualism has also been simulated (Lipowska, 2011; Roberts, 2012). Cultural evolution can be captured by horizontal communication between individuals in the same generation or vertical communication from adults to children. The latter typically lets the agents breed, age and die, with the iterated learning model (Smith et al., 2003) being popular.

A variety of language games exist, from simple naming games, where the agents' only topic concerns one specific object (Lipowska, 2011), to more cognitive grounding games (Steels and Loetzsch, 2012). There have also been studies on some more complex types of interaction, such as spatial games (Spranger, 2013), factual description games (van Trijp, 2012) and action games (Steels and Spranger, 2009), where the agent communication is about objects in a physical environment, about real-world events, and about motoric behaviors, respectively.

3 The Baldwin effect in a naming game

Several researchers have created simulations to investigate the Baldwin effect, starting with Hinton and Nowlan (1987). Cangelosi and Parisi (2002) simulate agents who evolve a simple grammatical language in order to survive in a world filled with edible and poisonous mushrooms. Munroe and Cangelosi (2002) used this model to pursue the Baldwin effect, with partially blind agents initially having to learn features of edible mushrooms, but with the learned abilities getting more and more assimilated into the genome over the generations. Chater et al. (2009) argue that only stable parts of language *may* assimilate into the genetic makeup, while variation within the linguistic environment is too unstable to be a target of natural selection. Watanabe et al. (2008) use a similar model, but in contrast state that genetic assimilation not necessarily requires a stable linguistic environment.

Lipowska (2011) has pursued the Baldwin effect in a simple naming game model with the intention of mixing up a language game in a simulation that incorporates both learning, cultural and biological evolution. The model places a set of agents in a square lattice of a linear size L, where every agent is allowed — by a given probability p — to communicate with a random neighbor.

At each time step, a random agent is chosen and p initially decides whether the agent is allowed to communicate or will face a "population update". Every agent has an internal lexicon of N words with associated weights ($w_j : 1 \leq j \leq N$). Whenever a chosen speaker is to utter a word, the agent selects a word i from its lexicon with the probability $w_i / \sum_{j=1}^{N} w_j$. If the lexicon is empty ($N = 0$), a word is made up. A random neighbor in the lattice is then chosen as the hearer. If both agents know the uttered word, the dialog is deemed a success, and if not, a failure. Upon success, both agents increase the uttered word's weight in their lexica by a learning ability variable. Each agent k is equipped with such a variable l ($0 < l_k < 1$). This learning ability is meant to, in its simplicity, reflect the genetic assimilation.

Instead of engaging in communication, the chosen agent is occasionally updated, by a probability $1 - p$. Agents die or survive with a probability p_s which is given by an equation that takes into account age, knowledge (lexicon weights in respect to the population's average weights), and simulation arguments. If the agent has a high-weighted lexicon and is young of age, and therefore survives at a given time step, the agent is allowed to breed if there are empty spaces in its neighborhood.

All in all, each time step can terminate with eight different scenarios: in addition to the two communication scenarios (success or failure), the scenario where the agent dies, as well as the one where the agents lives but only has non-empty neighbors (so that no change is possible), there are four possibilities for breeding. If the agent breeds, the off-spring either inherit the parent's learning ability or gain a new learning ability, with a probability p_m. With the same mutation probability, the off-spring also either gains a new word or inherits the parent's highest-weight word.

This model was implemented with the aim to reproduce Lipowska's results. She argues that her model is fairly robust to both population size and her given arguments; however, our experiments do not support this: as the Baldwin effect unfold, it does not follow the same abrupt course as in Lipowska's model. This could be due to some assumptions that had to be made, since Lipowska (2011), for instance, presents no details on how age is calculated. We thus assume that every time an agent is allowed to communicate, its age gets incremented. Another possibility could be to increment every agent's age at every time step, so that agents get older even if they do not communicate. Furthermore, the initial values for learnability are not clearly stated. Lipowska uses several different values in her analysis. We have used 0.5, which makes a decrease in learnability a part of the evolutionary search space as well.

Simulations with parameters similar to those used by Lipowska (2011) [$iterations = 200,000$, $mutation_{chance} = 0.01, L = 25, p = 0.4, l = 0.5$], produce results as in Figure 1, showing the highest weighted word per agent after 50k and 150k time steps, with each agent being a dot in a "heat map"; black dots indicate dead agents (empty space). The number of groups are reduced over time, and their sizes grow, as more agents agree on a lexicon and as favorable mutations spread through the population, (as indicated by agent learnability; Figure 2). Even after 200k iterations, consensus is not reached (which it was in Lipowska's simulation), but the agent population agrees on one word if the simulation is allowed to run further. It is natural to assume that the difference lays in the details of how age is calculated, as noted above.

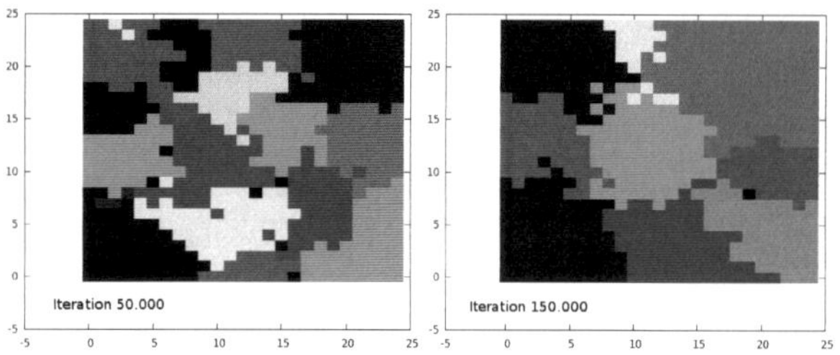

Figure 1: Ca 16 different words dominate the population at iteration 50k and nine at iteration 150k.

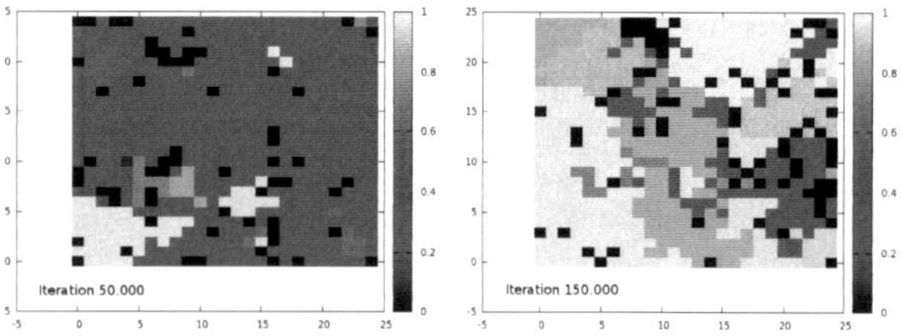

Figure 2: Mutations favoring learnability at iteration 50k spread substantially by iteration 150k.

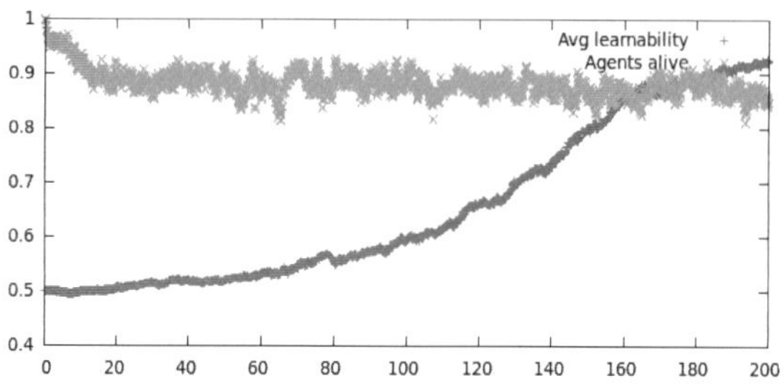

Figure 3: Fraction of agents alive in the lattice and average learnability in the population (s-shaped).

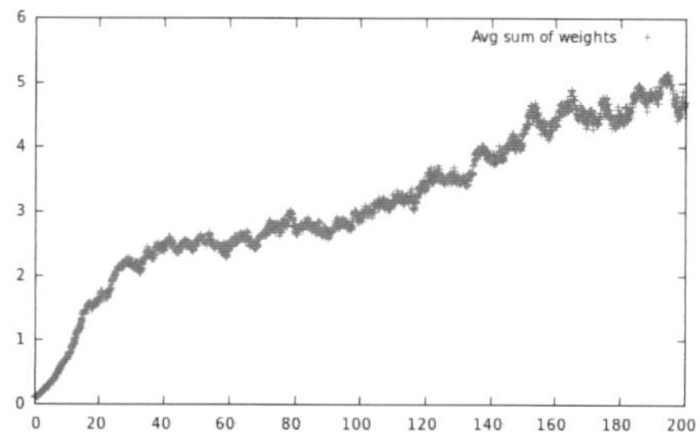

Figure 4: Average sum of weights in agent lexica.

Diverting from Lipowska's parameters and skewing towards faster turnover (higher mutation rate, higher possibility of survival with richer lexicon/higher age, etc.), gives behavior similar to hers, with faster and more abrupt genetic assimilation, as shown Figure 3. The upper line in the figure represents the fraction of agents alive in the lattice. It is initially fully populated, but the population decreases with time and balances at a point where death and birth are equally tensioned.

Agents with higher learnability tend to live longer, and the lower graph in Figure 3 shows the average learnability in the population. It is roughly sigmoid (S-shaped; cf. Lipowska's experiment) as a result of slow mutation rate in the first phase, followed by a phase with rapid mutation rate (ca 100k–170k) as the learnability also gets inherited, and decreasing rate towards the end when mutations are more likely to ruin agent learnability (when the learning ability l is at its upper limit). As can be seen in Figure 4, the agents rapidly get to a stable weighted lexicon before the Baldwin effect shows itself around time step 100k.

As mentioned, Lipowska's model did not reflect the robustness argued in her paper: for other values of p, the number of empty spots in the population lattice starts to diverge substantially, and for some values all agents simply die. As population sizes vary, the number of iterations must also be adjusted to get similar results. If not, the agents will not reach the same population turn-over as for smaller population sizes since only one agent may be updated per iteration. Lipowska (2011) compensated with higher mutation rate on simulations with different population sizes; however, these could be two variables somewhat more independent of each other. The model would have been much more stable if it contained aspects of a typical genetic algorithm, where agents are allowed to interact freely within generations. This way, the model could be acting more upon natural selection (and in search of the Baldwin effect), instead of relying on well-chosen parameters to work.

4 Discussion and future work

Language is a complex adaptive system with numerous variables to consider. Thus we must make a number of assumptions when studying language and its evolution, and can only investigate certain aspects at a time through simplifications and abstractions. As this paper has concentrated on the agent-based models of the field, many studies reflecting such other aspects had to be left out.

In addition, there has lately been a lot of work studying small adjustments to the agent-based models, in order to make them more realistic by, for example, having multiple hearers in a language game conversations (Li et al., 2013), different topologies (Lei et al., 2010; Lipowska and Lipowski, 2012), and more heterogeneous populations (Gong et al., 2006).

In general, though, simulations on language evolution tend to have relatively small and fixed sizes (Baronchelli et al., 2006; Vogt, 2007) — and few studies seem to take social dynamics (Gong et al., 2008; Kalampokis et al., 2007) or geography into account (Patriarca and Heinsalu, 2009).

Further work is still needed to make existing models more realistic and to analyze relations between different models (e.g., by combining them). Biological evolution could be studied with more flexible (or plastic) neural networks. Cultural evolution could be investigated under more realistic geographical and demographical influence, while learning could be analyzed even further in light of social dynamics, as different linguistic phenomena unfold. Quillinan (2006) presented a model concerning how a network of social relationships could evolve with language traits. This model could be taken further in combination with existing language games or it could be used to show how language responds to an exposure of continuous change in a complex social network.

Notably, many present models have a rather naïve way of selecting cultural parents, and a genetic algorithm for giving fitness to agents in terms of having (assimilated) the best strategies for learning (e.g., memory efficiency), social conventions (e.g., emotions, popularity), and/or simple or more advanced grammar could be explored.

A particular path we aim to pursue is to study a language game with a simple grammar under social influence (e.g., with populations in different fixed and non-fixed graphs, with multiple hearers), contained within a genetic algorithm. In such a setting, the agents must come up with strategies for spreading and learning new languages, and need to develop fault-tolerant models for speaking with close and distant neighbors. This could be a robust model where a typical language game could be examined, in respect to both biological and cultural evolution, with a more realistic perspective.

Acknowledgments

We would like thank the three anonymous reviewers for several very useful comments. Thanks also to Keith Downing for providing feedback on work underlying this article.

The third author is supported by a grant from the Norwegian University of Science and Technology. Part of this work was funded by the PRESEMT project (EC grant number FP7-ICT-4-248307).

References

James Mark Baldwin. 1896. A new factor in evolution. *The American Naturalist*, 30(354):441–451.

Andrea Baronchelli, Maddalena Felici, Vittorio Loreto, Emanuele Caglioti, and Luc Steels. 2006. Sharp transition towards shared vocabularies in multi-agent systems. *Journal of Statistical Mechanics: Theory and Experiment*, 2006(06):P06014.

Andrea Baronchelli, Nick Chater, Romualdo Pastor-Satorras, and Morten H. Christiansen. 2012. The biological origin of linguistic diversity. *PLoS ONE*, 7(10):e48029.

Joris Bleys and Luc Steels. 2011. Linguistic selection of language strategies. In G. Kampis, I. Karsai, and E. Szathmáry, editors, *Advances in Artificial Life. Darwin Meets von Neumann*, volume 2, pages 150–157. Springer.

Angelo Cangelosi and Domenico Parisi. 2002. Computer simulation: A new scientific approach to the study of language evolution. In Angelo Cangelosi and Domenico Parisi, editors, *Simulating the Evolution of Language*, chapter 1, pages 3–28. Springer, London.

Nick Chater, Florencia Reali, and Morten H Christiansen. 2009. Restrictions on biological adaptation in language evolution. *Proceedings of the National Academy of Sciences*, 106(4):1015–1020.

Noam Chomsky. 1986. *Knowledge of language: Its nature, origins, and use*. Greenwood.

Morten H. Christiansen and Simon Kirby. 2003. Language evolution: consensus and controversies. *TRENDS in Cognitive Sciences*, 7(7):300–307.

Rick Dale and Gary Lupyan. 2012. Understanding the origins of morphological diversity: the linguistic niche hypothesis. *Advances in Complex Systems*, 15(03n04):1150017.

Terrence W. Deacon. 2010. A role for relaxed selection in the evolution of the language capacity. *Proceedings of the National Academy of Sciences*, 107(Supplement 2):9000–9006.

Nicholas Evans and Stephen C. Levinson. 2009. The myth of language universals: Language diversity and its importance for cognitive science. *Behavioral and Brain Sciences*, 32(05):429–448.

Tao Gong and Lan Shuai. 2013. Computer simulation as a scientific approach in evolutionary linguistics. *Language Sciences*, 40:12–23.

Tao Gong, James W. Minett, and William S-Y Wang. 2006. Language origin and the effects of individuals popularity. In *Proceedings of the 2006 IEEE Congress on Evolutionary Computation*, pages 999–1006, Vancouver, British Columbia, Jul. IEEE.

Tao Gong, James W. Minett, and William S-Y Wang. 2008. Exploring social structure effect on language evolution based on a computational model. *Connection Science*, 20(2-3):135–153.

Geoffrey E Hinton and Steven J Nowlan. 1987. How learning can guide evolution. *Complex systems*, 1(3):495–502.

Edward Kako. 1999. Elements of syntax in the systems of three language-trained animals. *Animal Learning & Behavior*, 27(1):1–14.

Alkiviadis Kalampokis, Kosmas Kosmidis, and Panos Argyrakis. 2007. Evolution of vocabulary on scale-free and random networks. *Physica A: Statistical Mechanics and its Applications*, 379(2):665 – 671.

Simon Kirby. 2002. Natural language from artificial life. *Artificial Life*, 8(2):185–215.

Richard G. Klein. 2008. Out of Africa and the evolution of human behavior. *Evolutionary Anthropology: Issues, News, and Reviews*, 17(6):267–281.

Chuang Lei, Jianyuan Jia, Te Wu, and Long Wang. 2010. Coevolution with weights of names in structured language games. *Physica A: Statistical Mechanics and its Applications*, 389(24):5628–5634.

Bing Li, Guanrong Chen, and Tommy W.S. Chow. 2013. Naming game with multiple hearers. *Communications in Nonlinear Science and Numerical Simulation*, 18(5):1214–1228.

Dorota Lipowska and Adam Lipowski. 2012. Naming game on adaptive weighted networks. *Artificial Life*, 18(3):311–323.

Dorota Lipowska. 2011. Naming game and computational modelling of language evolution. *Computational Methods in Science and Technology*, 17(1–2):41–51.

Steve Munroe and Angelo Cangelosi. 2002. Learning and the evolution of language: the role of cultural variation and learning costs in the Baldwin effect. *Artificial Life*, 8(4):311–339.

Mark Pagel. 2000. The history, rate and pattern of world linguistic evolution. In Ch. Knight, J.R. Hurford, and M. Studdert-Kennedy, editors, *The Evolutionary Emergence of Language: Social Function and the Origins of Linguistic Form*, chapter 22, pages 391–416. Cambridge University Press.

Marco Patriarca and Els Heinsalu. 2009. Influence of geography on language competition. *Physica A: Statistical Mechanics and its Applications*, 388(2–3):174–186.

Steven Pinker and Paul Bloom. 1990. Natural language and natural selection. *Behavioral and Brain Sciences*, 13:707–784.

Andrea Puglisi, Andrea Baronchelli, and Vittorio Loreto. 2008. Cultural route to the emergence of linguistic categories. *Proceedings of the National Academy of Sciences*, 105(23):7936–7940.

Justin Quillinan. 2006. Social networks and cultural transmission. Master of Science Thesis, School of Philosophy, Psychology and Language Sciences, University of Edinburgh, Edinburgh, Scotland, Aug.

Sean Geraint Roberts. 2012. *An evolutionary approach to bilingualism*. Ph.D. thesis, School of Philosophy, Psychology and Language Sciences, University of Edinburgh, Edinburgh, Scotland, Oct.

George Gaylord Simpson. 1953. The Baldwin effect. *Evolution*, 7(2):110–117.

Kenny Smith, Simon Kirby, and Henry Brighton. 2003. Iterated learning: A framework for the emergence of language. *Artificial Life*, 9(4):371–386.

Michael Spranger. 2013. Evolving grounded spatial language strategies. *KI-Künstliche Intelligenz*, 27(2):1–10.

Luc Steels and Martin Loetzsch. 2012. The grounded naming game. In L. Steels, editor, *Experiments in Cultural Language Evolution*, pages 41–59. John Benjamins.

Luc Steels and Michael Spranger. 2009. How experience of the body shapes language about space. In *Proceedings of the 21st International Joint Conference on Artificial Intelligence*, pages 14–19, Pasadena, California, Jul. IJCAI.

Luc Steels. 1995. A self-organizing spatial vocabulary. *Artificial Life*, 2(3):319–332.

Luc Steels. 2011. Modeling the cultural evolution of language. *Physics of Life Reviews*, 8(4):339–356.

Ian Tattersall. 2010. Human evolution and cognition. *Theory in Biosciences*, 129(2–3):193–201.

Remi van Trijp. 2012. The evolution of case systems for marking event structure. In L. Steels, editor, *Experiments in Cultural Language Evolution*, pages 169–205. John Benjamins.

Paul Vogt. 2007. Group size effects on the emergence of compositional structures in language. In F. Almeida e Costa, L.M. Rocha, E. Costa, I Harvey, and A. Coutinho, editors, *Advances in Artificial Life: Proceedings of the 9th European Conference (ECAL 2007)*, pages 405–414, Lisbon, Portugal, Sep. Springer.

Yusuke Watanabe, Reiji Suzuki, and Takaya Arita. 2008. Language evolution and the Baldwin effect. *Artificial Life and Robotics*, 12(1-2):65–69.

Missing Generalizations: A Supervised Machine Learning Approach to L2 Written Production

Daniel Wiechmann
Amsterdam Center for Language and Communication
University of Amsterdam
d.wiechmann@uva.nl

Elma Kerz
Department of English Linguistics
RWTH Aachen University
kerz@anglistik.rwth-aachen.de

Abstract

Recent years have witnessed a growing interest in *usage-based* models of language, which characterize linguistic knowledge in terms of emerging generalizations derived from experience with language via processes of similarity-based distributional analysis and analogical reasoning. Language learning then involves building the *right* generalizations, i.e. the recognition and recreation of the statistical regularities underlying the target language. Focusing on the domain of relativization, this study examines to what extent the generalizations of advanced second language learners pertaining to the usage of complex constructions differ from those of experts in written production. We approach this question through supervised machine learning employing as a primary modeling tool random forests with conditional inference trees as base learners.

1 Introduction

One of the central questions in second (L2) language learning is how L2 learners construct a new language system on the basis of only limited exposure to the target language. While formalist (*generative, syntax-based*) approaches have emphasized the reliance on innate mechanisms and principles, functionalist (*emergentist, usage-based* (UB)) approaches have highlighted processes of bottom-up induction of grammatical knowledge from input by way of complex automatic distributional analyses of perceived utterances at many grain-sizes (cf. Harrington, 2010 for an overview). The capacity to detect statistical regularities in the perceived input and to exploit these for purposes of building up more abstract generalizations is at work not only in earlier stages of language acquisition, but remains throughout life (cf. Farmer, Fine & Jaeger, 2011), and is operative not only in the acquisition of L1 but also L2 (see, MacWhinney, 2013 for an overview). Grammatical knowledge then emerges through iterative categorization, in which the categories formed by grouping together similar exemplars at one level form the input of subsequent categorization processes at the next higher level of organization. In this view, language learning involves the task of identifying those variables that are involved in defining the generalizations that characterize conventional language use. In earlier stages of development, learners are found to establish generalizations along easily detectable, salient variables (MacWhinney, 2008). With growing experience, learners detect additional defining features and relationships among features and continue to refine their knowledge, resulting in their own productions become more and more target-like.

The resulting knowledge is likely to comprise both stored exemplars as well as generalizations derived through processes of analogical reasoning (see, e.g., Tomasello, 2003; Daelemans & van den Bosch, 2005; Goldberg, 2006; Ellis & Larsen-Freeman, 2009). At present, there is no general consensus as to what form the resulting knowledge takes and to what extent (if any) human linguistic knowledge is characterized by representational redundancy (cf. Wiechmann. Kerz. Snider & Jaeger, 2013 for a recent overview). Theoretical constructs to capture the units of linguistic regularity resulting from such processes of inductive learning include *local associations* and *memorized chunks* (Ellis, 2002), *computational routines* (O'Grady,

2005), and *constructions* (Tomasello, 2003; Goldberg, 2006; Langacker, 2008). In this paper, we assume the latter and follow a *UB constructionist* approach, in which all linguistic knowledge is characterized in terms of pairings of form and meaning, so called *constructions*. In this view, language learning concerns the emergence of symbolic units from the intricate interplay between "the memories of all the utterances a learner's entire history of language use and the frequency-biased abstraction of regularities within them" (Ellis and Freeman, 2009:92). The emerging constructional patterns assume various degrees of abstraction and internal complexity and range from morphemes, to words and idiomatic expressions, to partially schematic (Kay and Fillmore, 1999) to fully schematic constructional patterns, such as clause-level argument structure constructions (Goldberg, 2006). Constructionist accounts are thus committed to the belief that "[a]n adequate model of human language processing must allow for a heterogeneous store of elementary units, ranging from single words, and basic combinatory rules, to multiword constructions with various open slots and complete sentences" Beekhuizen, Bod & Zuidema (2013:267).

This study investigates knowledge about patterns at the sentential level, specifically knowledge about complex constructions involving relative clauses (henceforth RCs). RCs have played a pivotal role in the development of modern psycholinguistic theorizing and a lot of attention has been devoted to studying their acquisition and online processing (cf. Sheldon, 1974; Goodluck and Tavakolian, 1982; Diessel, 2004; Rohde, Levy & Kehler, 2011; Levy & Gibson, 2013; *inter alia*). In the domain of first language acquisition, UB constructionist accounts have portrayed the development of relative constructions types in terms of *clause expansion*, i.e. in terms of gradual transformations of simple (non-embedded) sentences into multiple-clause units (cf. Diessel & Tomasello, 2000; Tomasello, 2003; Diessel, 2004). In the domain of L2 learning, research on relativization has generally focused on assessing the degree to which L2 learning reflects the developmental pathways of L1 learning (Gass, 1979; Doughty, 1991; Abdomanafi & Rezaee, 2012). Largely based on comprehension tasks, these studies investigated if the learner proficiency in RCs decreases at lower positions of the accessibility hierarchy (Keenan and Comrie, 1977) and/or investigated related proposals revolving around the internal syntax of relative clauses (e.g. the *Non-Interruption Hypothesis*, Slobin, 1973; the *Parallel Function Hypothesis*, Sheldon, 1974, or the *Perceptual Difficulty Hypothesis*, Kuno, 1975). This research has primarily addressed questions targeted at beginning and/or intermediate stages of L2 development of RCs. In recent years, there has been an increased interest in advanced stages L2 learning and harder to detect aspects of linguistic knowledge, which has resulted in a shift towards written production as "[…] in writing, rather than in speaking, the learner can […] better show what he or she is capable of doing in and with L2 because writing allows far more reflection and is therefore usually somewhat more complex linguistically than speaking" Verspoor, Schmid and Xu (2010:239). A growing availability of learner corpora of advanced L2 written productions gave rise to a number of studies whose main aim was to reveal factors of "foreign-soundingness even in the absence of downright errors" (Granger 2004:132). It was shown that - irrespective of their L1 background - advanced L2 learners face similar challenges on their way to near-native proficiency (DeKeyser, 2005; Wiechmann & Kerz, 2014) in connection with (a) a lack of register awareness and (b) an incomplete understanding of the complex probabilistic regularities underlying optional linguistic phenomena, which typically includes the integration of generalizations from various levels of organization (lexical, structural, discourse-pragmatic, etc.).

Focusing on advanced L2 learners' written productions, the present study sets out to investigate a complex domain of grammar, viz. relativization. Specifically, we seek to understand the conditions in which experts prefer a reduced, non-finite RC over a more explicit, finite RC. The examples in (1) to (4) - taken from our expert data - illustrate the target structures. The modified nominal in the MC is referred to as the *head* of the RC.

(1) The [$_{\text{head}}$ results]] [$_{\text{RC}}$ that/which are shown in Tables IV and V] add to the picsture […]
(2) The [$_{\text{head}}$ results] [$_{\text{RC}}$ shown in Tables IV and V] add to the picture […]
(3) The [$_{\text{head}}$ factors] [$_{\text{RC}}$ that/which are contributing to the natural destruction of microbes] [...]

(4) The [$_{head}$ factors] [$_{RC}$ contributing to the natural destruction of microbes] [...]

We focus on the register of academic writing as it is characterized by a very condensed style (cf. Biber and Gray, 2010), which invites the increased usage of non-finite RCs. Furthermore, highly specialized domains, such as academic writing, afford specific register-contingent constructions (Kerz & Wiechmann, accepted).

2 Data

The data were retrieved from a corpus of 20 term papers produced by German students of English linguistics at RWTH Aachen University in their second and third year of study (N_{words} ~ 80,000) and a same-sized control expert corpus of 10 peer-reviewed articles appearing in various journals on language studies. Manual extraction of all subject RC gave rise to a set of roughly 1,500 data points, of which 713 instances were produced by learners and 793 were produced by experts. All instances were manually annotated with respect to eight variables that have been shown to affect the online processing of RC constructions (cf. Fox and Thompson, 1990; Wiechmann, 2010 for a comprehensive discussion).

Variable	Description	Values
GROUP	item sampled from which group	advanced learner / expert
ID	source text	10 sources expert writing, 20 sources advanced learners
FINITE.RC	finiteness of RC	finite / non-finite
EXT.SYN	modified nominal in the MC	SU, DO, PN (predicate nominal), lower
LENGTH.BIN	length of sentence in words	dichotomized around the mean
ADD.MOD	presence of additional modifier (AP or PP)	yes / no
HEAD.TYPE	morphosyntactic type of head	lexical, pronominal, proper name
DEFINITE.HEAD	definiteness of head noun	definite / indefinite
ANIMACY.HEAD	animacy of head noun	animate / inanimate
GENERIC.HEAD	contentfulness of head noun	generic / specific
FREQUENT.AC	element of 100 most frequent heads in register (COCA/BNC)	yes / no

Table 1: Variables used in data description

The variables in Table 1 concern features of (a) the overall sentence (e.g. which grammatical role in the main clause is being modified by way of an RC, how long is the overall sentence, etc.) and (b) features of the head of the RC (e.g. does it refer to an animate or inanimate referent, is the nominal definite of indefinite, etc.).

3 Method

To assess to what extent the learners have successfully captured the regularities underlying the target system, we fit classification models to each data set that were geared to discriminate between finite or non-finite RC constructions based on the distributional information about the variables listed in Table 1. If learners have indeed successfully induced the right generalizations, then the models should reveal similar structures for both experts and learners. As a primary modeling tool, we used a random forest (RF) technique utilizing conditional inference trees as base learners (for details, cf. Hothorn, Hornik, & Zeileis, 2006; Strobl, Boulesteix, Kneib, Augustin, & Zeileis, 2008; Strobl, Hothorn, Zeileis, 2009). We focused on this ensemble method for its ability to (a) produce reliable estimates of variable importance in scenarios of correlating predictors (Belsley et al., 1980) – which are the norm rather than the exception for linguistic choice phenomena like the one investigated here –, (b) for its ability to avoid biases towards categorical variables that have more levels, and (c) for their ease of interpretability. The criterion for stopping of an individual tree's growth was based on multiplicity Bonferroni adjusted p-values from permutation tests suggested in Strasser & Weber (1999). Recursion was stopped when a hypothesis of independence could not be rejected at $\alpha = 0.05$. We evaluated the RF model on the basis of classification accuracy via repeated random sub-sampling validation (100 iterations; random split: 70% training data – 30% test data) and compared its performance with a logistic regression model (GLM) including only main effects and a support vector machine (SVM) with an RBF kernel. Average classification accuracy for the expert data ranged from 69% for the GLM, to 70% for the RF technique to 72% for the SVM. The performance of identical models on the learner data was about 5% higher on average. To estimate the degree of heterogeneity of the RC productions that is due to individual author(s) and L2 learners respectively, we also fit

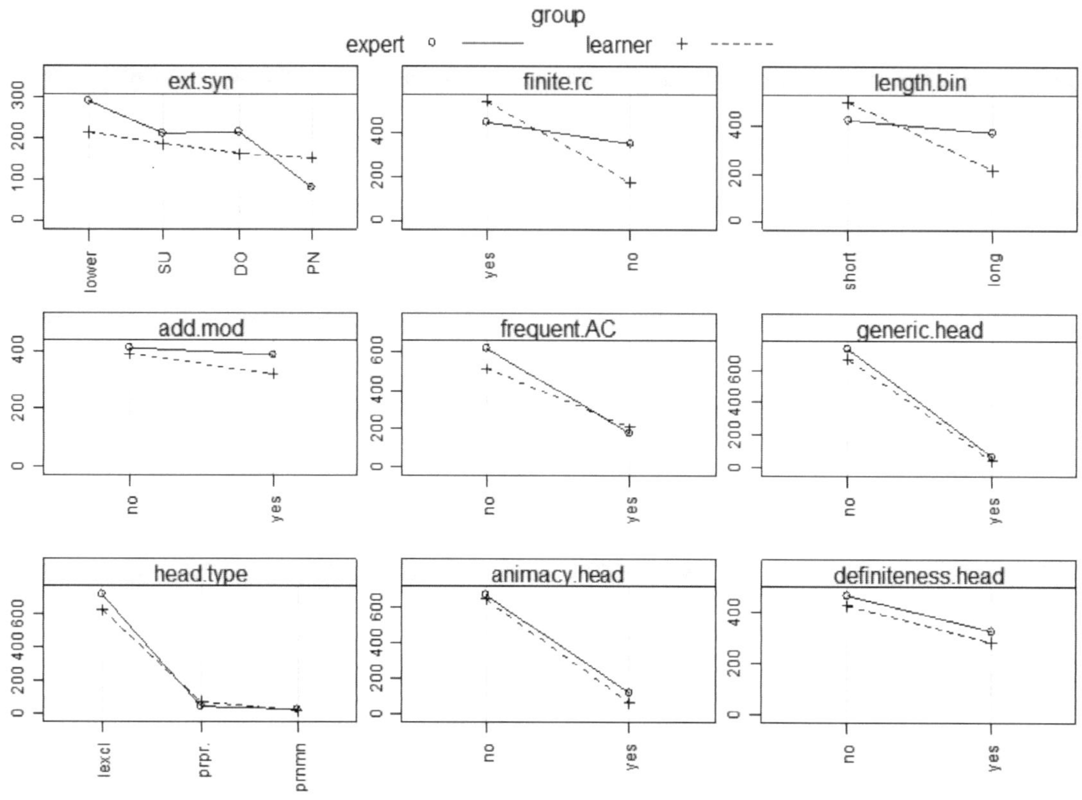

Figure 1: Distributions RC features: learners vs. experts

generalized linear mixed models (GLMM) to the data that in addition to the variables of interest also contained the variable ID (indicating the source text) as a random effect and investigated the adjustments to the intercept as an estimate of the degree of heterogeneity of the RC productions.

4 Results

Figure 1 presents an overview of the distributions of the descriptive variables in expert and learner productions.

4.1 Target-like productions

Figure 2 presents the results of a single conditional inference tree fit to all available data points from the expert set. In this model, the most important variable concerns the animacy of the head of the RC: in target-like productions, non-finite variants are more likely to be chosen when the modified nominal is inanimate (split at Node 1). Within the set of modifications of inanimate head nouns (Node 2), RCs non-finite variants are strongly preferred when the modified nominal functions as the subject of the dominating clause (Node 4). Within the subset of non-subject modifications, the likelihood of an RC to be non-finite is greater when it is definite (Node 5). The model asserts additional structure with reference to the external syntax of the RC and the presence of an additional modifier to create a total of eleven partitions before tree growth is stopped. As individual trees are susceptible to small changes in the data, which typically leads to trees exhibiting high degrees of variability in their predictions, we checked the structure reported in Figure 2 against the relative variable importance derived from 500 trees with three variables randomly sampled as candidates at each node. Following Strobl, Malley and Tutz (2009), we considered variables to be non-important if their importance is negative, zero or has a small positive value that lies in the same range as the negative values The RF model supports the important roles of all variables in the reported tree (relative importance in ascending order: FREQUENT.AC -0.002, HEAD.TYPE: 0.002, GENERIC.HEAD: 0.004, LENGTH: 0.005, ADD.MOD: 0.013, EXT.SYN: 0.013, DEFINITENESS.HEAD: 0.018, ANIMACY.HEAD: 0.036). We next estimated the variation that is due to individual stylistic differences in the ten texts that constitute our

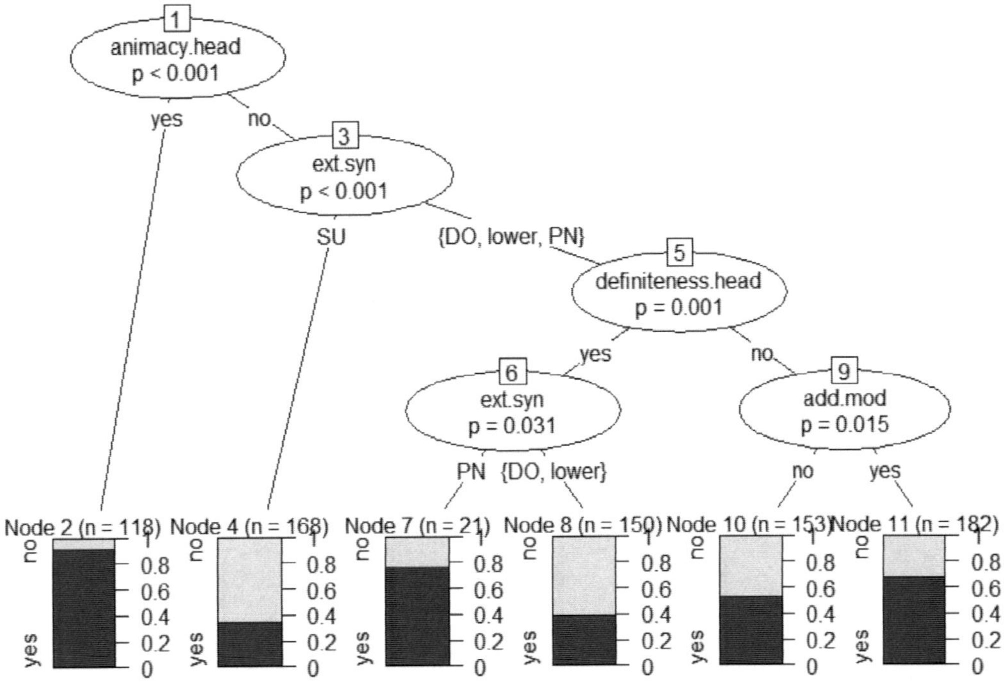

Figure 2: Conditional inference tree for expert data. Nodes contain Bonferroni-adjusted P-values (alpha = 0.05 as stopping criterion)

expert data using a GLLM that contained ID (source text) as a random effect. To avoid unnecessary model complexity, we excluded FREQUENT.AC, which was demonstrably unimportant for the constructional choice. As shown in Table 2, all effects were statistically significant at $\alpha = 0.05$ (no 2-way nor 3-way interactions was significant at $\alpha = 0.05$). The variability in the intercept between the texts in the expert corpus is negligible, suggesting that the relationships between the variables are rather robust in the target register (ID intercept variance = 0.07, SD = 0.26). Figure 3 shows the conditional modes of the random effect ID.

	Coef	SE	z	Pr(>|z|)
(Intercept)	0.31	0.21	1.45	0.15
ANIMATE.HEAD – no:yes	2.38	0.36	6.64	0.00
EXT.SYN – DO:lower	-0.12	0.20	-0.62	0.53
EXT.SYN – DO:PN	0.57	0.30	1.89	0.06
EXT.SYN – DO:SU	-0.48	0.22	-2.16	0.03
HEAD.TYPE – lex:pron	0.69	0.87	0.80	0.42
HEAD.TYPE – lex:name	0.91	0.38	2.38	0.02
LENGTH – long:short	-0.43	0.16	-2.68	0.01
ADD.MOD – no:yes	0.43	0.16	2.62	0.01
GENERIC.HEAD – no:yes	1.15	0.41	2.77	0.01
DEFINITE.HEAD – no:yes	-0.73	0.17	-4.24	0.00

Table 2: Generalized linear mixed logit model fit by the Laplace approximation (expert data)

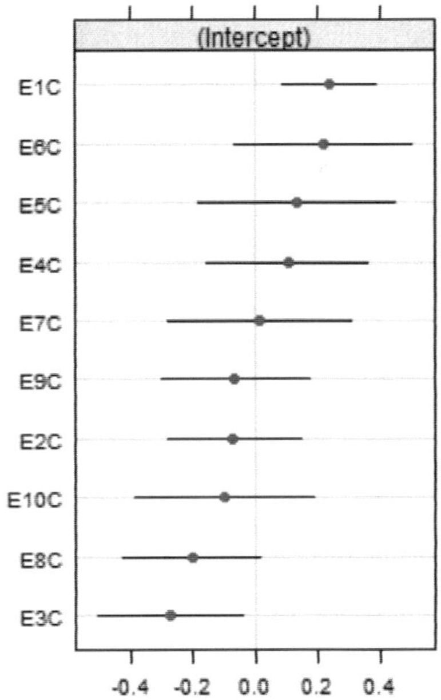

Figure 3: Conditional modes for the random effect ID in GLMM fit to expert data

4.2 Learner productions

We applied the exact same procedure to the learner data. We first present the results of a tree-based model fit to all exemplars in the learner

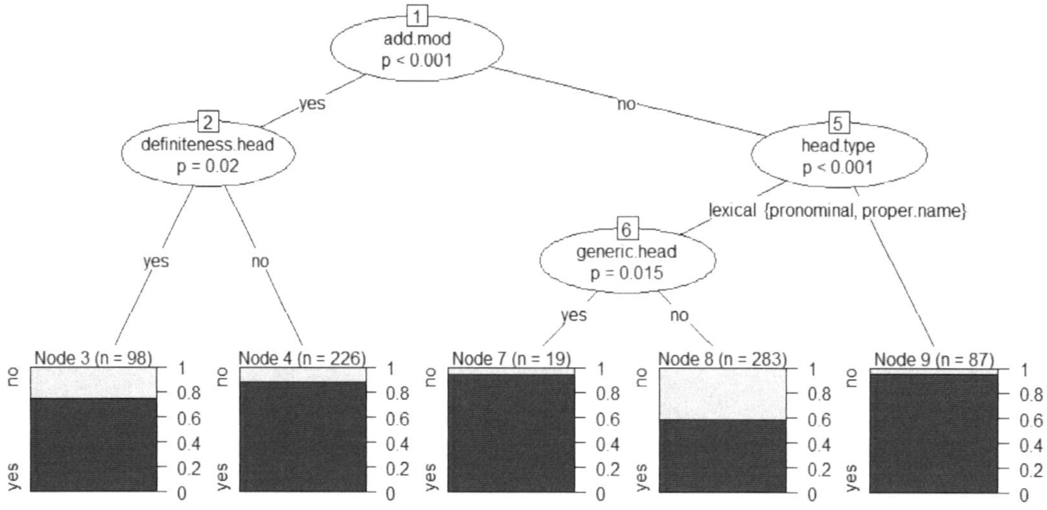

Figure 4: Conditional inference tree for learner data. Nodes contain Bonferroni-adjusted P-values (alpha = 0.05 as stopping criterion)

data (Figure 4). We found that the structure underlying the learner data is (a) simpler than the expert structure and also (b) different than the expert structure. At the top level, the data are split relative to whether or not there is an additional element to modify the head noun: the likelihood of a non-finite RC is slightly greater in the presence of an additional modifier and in particular with lexical heads that are not generic. The variable importance estimates derived from a model comprising 500 trees supported the importance of ADD.MOD, DEFINITENESS.HEAD, and HEAD.TYPE but not the importance of GENERIC.HEAD (relative importance in ascending order: GENERIC.HEAD = 0.002, ANIMACY.HEAD = 0.003, FREQUENT.AC = 0.003, LENGTH = 0.003, EXT.SYN = 0.004, DEFINITENESS.HEAD = 0.006, HEAD.TYPE = 0.006, ADD.MOD = 0.0205). The GLMM presented an overall similar picture supporting the importance of GENERIC.HEAD.

	Coef	SE	z	Pr(>|z|)
(Intercept)	0.92	0.36	2.52	0.01
ANIMATE.HEAD – no:yes	-0.32	0.38	-0.85	0.40
EXT.SYN – DO:lower	0.05	0.29	0.15	0.88
EXT.SYN – DO:PN	0.02	0.32	0.05	0.96
EXT.SYN – DO:SU	-0.25	0.30	-0.85	0.39
HEAD.TYPE – lex:pron	0.79	1.25	0.63	0.53
HEAD.TYPE – lex:name	3.70	0.77	4.81	0.00
LENGTH – long:short	-0.12	0.23	-0.52	0.60
ADD.MOD – no:yes	1.14	0.21	5.33	0.00
GENERIC.HEAD – no:yes	3.42	1.16	2.94	0.00
DEFINITE.HEAD – no:yes	-0.67	0.23	-2.94	0.00

Table 3: Generalized linear mixed logit model fit by the Laplace approximation (learner data)

Furthermore, the variability in the intercept between learners is a more pronounced than that of the experts (Figure 5).

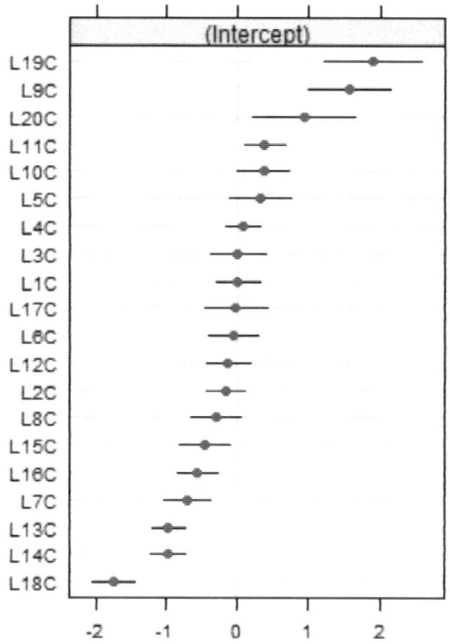

Figure 5: Conditional modes for the random effect ID in GLMM fit to learner data

5 Discussion

Our results indicated that advanced learners have clearly not yet built up the generalizations that characterize expert productions of non-finite RC constructions: firstly, the learners clearly underused non-finite variants of RCs relative to finite ones as evidenced by an observed ratio of finite RC to non-finite RC of roughly 2:1 in learner language (compared to almost even proportions in expert language). As learners typically seek to maximize the transfer of knowledge from their L1 (MacWhinney, 2013), we assume that the underuse is at least partly due to the fact that there is no transferrable isomorphic translational equivalent to English nonfinite RCs in their L1 (German). However, this assessment clearly goes beyond the available evidence and falls outside the scope of this study. Secondly, our learners have derived generalizations that are less complex than those characterizing expert productions. Thirdly, they have assigned too much importance to some generalizations, e.g. the role of additional modifiers, and too little importance to others, e.g. animacy of the head noun and the external syntax of the RC. A linguistic analysis of relative constructions, which we will sketch only very briefly here, revealed that all variables to distinguish non-finite from finite subject relatives in expert language are semantically motivated. For example, in expert language non-finite RCs were strongly preferred in contexts where the RC modifies an inanimate, definite, lexical head that is the grammatical subject of the main clause as in (5).

(5) The logic [used to resolve errors here] comes from the Cancellation/ Domination Lemma of Prince and Smolensky (1993:148) [...]

In such contexts the RC is almost invariably non-restrictive, i.e. its function is not to restrict the set of possible referents of the nominal, but rather to attribute a secondary predication to an already established discourse referent, while the main predication about that referent is encoded on the main clause (Wiechmann, 2010). The marginal adjustments to the intercept in the GLLM fit to the expert data suggested that the effects of these variables on the choice of RC are robust in the target register. In contrast, none of the constitutive features of this construction characterized non-finite RCs in learner language. The variable to distinguish the contrasted structural realizations of RCs in learner language most strongly was the presence of an additional modifier. An RC modifying a nominal that contains further pre- or post-modification was more likely to be realized in full finite form. Closer inspection of the data suggested that this preference does not reflect a semantic motivation but rather reflects the tendency of language users to prefer explicit variants over reduced ones in contexts of greater complexity (Rohdenburg, 2003). Outside the context of semantically motivated constructions, expert language exhibited this preference as well, but its effect on the structural choice was noticeably less pronounced. We also found that the variability in the intercept is not very high suggesting that the generalizability of our findings is not threatened by the variability of the subjects' abilities to identify relevant generalizations. We found that about 80% of the learners formed a rather homogeneous group resulting in marginal adjustments to the intercept.

On a methodological note, we would like to briefly address two points: First, our approach to investigate (missing) generalizations does not speak to the issue of what exactly are the productive units in language and how exactly the operations of combinations are to be conceived of (for discussion cf. Bod 2009 and references therein) and does thus not constrain the computational realization of the statistical induction processes underlying language learning (cf. Clark, 2001; Klein and Manning, 2002; Zuidema, 2006; Bod & Smets, 2012; *inter alia*). In this paper, we were interested to what extent advanced L2 learners have succeeded in identifying generalizations pertaining to variables that figure in psycholinguistic accounts of sentence-level processing (e.g. animacy and definiteness of the head, type of embedding, etc.). Second, it was *not* the primary goal of our modeling to maximize predictive success. We address this point because we have also fit models based on much richer descriptions of the data (20+ variables) and some of these models reached levels of classification accuracy that exceeded that of the models reported here. However, we think that there are still good reasons to believe that their inclusion is actually detrimental to our attempts to understand the dynamics of language learning. To exemplify this: the variable 'voice of the RC' leads to an about 5% increase in classification accuracy of the expert model. However, its predictive value stems from the fact that it incorporates the effects of theoretically motivated variables thereby overshadowing their effects. Passive constructions tend to have inanimate subjects. As all RCs investigated here are subject relatives, this entails that the head of a passive RC tends to be inanimate. We find that 'voice of the RC' is more predictive than animacy of the head, but the causal structure of the theory would have it that head animacy affects voice, rather than the other way round. With few exceptions, e.g. Baayen, Hendrix, and Ramscar (2013) on the reification of distributional effects, this general issue of predictors being robustly significant while lacking theoretical motivation has in our view not received the amount of attention it deserves. More generally, considerations like these motivate a shift towards the employment of causal models (cf. Pearl 2009).

References

Seyed Jalal Abdolmanafi and Abdolbaghi Rezaee 2012. The difficulty hierarchy in the acquisition of English relative clauses. *International Journal of English and Education,* 1(2):170-179.

Harald R. H. Baayen, Peter Hendrix, and Michael Ramscar. 2013. Sidestepping the combinatorial explosion: Towards a processing model based on discriminative learning. *Language and Speech,* 56(3): 329-347.

Barend Beekhuizen, Rens Bod and Willem Zuidema. 2013. Three design principles of language: the search for parsimony and redundancy. *Language and Speech*, 56(3):265-290.

David Belsley, Edwin E. Kuh, and Roy E. Welsch. 1982. *Regression Diagnostics. Identifying Influential Data and Sources of Collinearity.* New York: John Wiley & Sons.

Douglas Biber and Bethany Gray. 2010. Challenging stereotypes about academic writing: complexity, elaboration, explicitness. *Journal of English for Academic Purposes,* 9:2-20.

Rens Bod. 2009. Constructions at Work or at Rest? *Cognitive Linguistics*, 20(1), 129–134.

Rens Bod and Margaux Smets, 2012. Empiricist Solutions to Nativist Problems using Tree-Substitution Grammars, *Proceedings Cognitive Models of Language Acquisition and Loss*, EACL 2012, Avignon, France, 10-18.

Alexander Clark. 2001. Unsupervised induction of stochastic context-free grammars using distributional clustering. Proceedings CoNLL 2001, 105–112.

Walter Daelemans, and Antal van den Bosch. 2005. *Memory-Based Language Processing.* Cambridge University Press, Cambridge, UK.

Robert DeKeyser. 2005. What makes learning second language grammar difficult? A review of issues. *Language Learning,* 55:1-25.

Holger Diessel. 2004. *The Acquisition of Complex Sentences.* Cambridge University Press, Cambridge.

Holger Diessel and Michael Tomasello. 2000. The development of relative clauses in spontaneous child speech. *Cognitive Linguistics,* 11:131-151.

Catherine Doughty. 1991. Second language instruction does make a difference: Evidence from an empirical study of SL relativization. *Studies in Second Language Acquisition,* 13(4):431-469.

Nick C. Ellis. 2002. Frequency effects in language processing. *Studies in Second Language Acquisition,* 24:143-188.

Nick C. Ellis & D. Larsen-Freeman. 2009. Constructing a second language: analyses and computational simulations of the emergence of linguistic constructions from usage. *Language Learning,* 59(1):93-128.

Thomas Farmer, Alex B. Fine & T. Florian Jaeger. 2011. Implicit context-specific learning leads to rapid shifts in syntactic expectations. In L. Carlson, C. Hoelscher & T.F. Shipley (eds.), *Proceedings of the 33rd Annual Meeting of the Cognitive Science Society,* pp. 2055-2061. Cognitive Science Society, Austin, TX.

Barbara Fox and Sandra A. Thompson. 1990. A discourse explanation of the grammar of relative clauses in English conversation. *Language,* 66:51-64.

Susan Gass. 1979. Language transfer and universal grammatical relations. *Language Transfer,* 29:327-452.

Adele Goldberg. 2006. *Constructions at Work: The Nature of Generalization in Language.* Oxford University Press, Oxford.

Helen Goodluck and Susan Tavakolian. 1982. Competence and processing in children's grammar of relative clauses. *Cognition,* 11:1-27.

Sylviane Granger. 2004. Computer learner corpus research: current status and future prospects. In U. Connor and T. Upton (eds.), *Computer Learner Corpora, Second Language Acquisition, and Foreign Language Teaching.* John Benjamins, Amsterdam, 3-33.

Michael Harrington. 2010. *Computational models of second language sentence processing.* In R. J. Kaplan (ed.), *Handbook of Applied Linguistics,* 2nd edition, pp. 189-204. Oxford University Press, Oxford, UK.

Torsten Hothorn, Kurt Hornik & Achim Zeileis. 2006. Unbiased recursive partitioning: A conditional inference framework. *Journal of Computational and Graphical Statistics,* 15(3): 651–674.

Paul Kay and Charles J. Fillmore. 1999. Grammatical constructions and linguistic generalizations: The *What's X doing Y?* construction. *Language,* 75:1-33.

Edward Keenan and Bernard Comrie. 1977. Noun phrase accessibility and Universal Grammar. *Linguistic Inquiry,* 8:63-99.

Elma Kerz and Daniel Wiechmann. accepted. Register-contingent entrenchment of constructional patterns: causal and concessive adverbial clauses in academic and newspaper writing. *Journal of English Linguistics*.

Dan Klein and Chris Manning. 2002. A general constituent-context model for improved grammar induction. *Proceedings ACL* 2002, Philadelphia, 128–135.

Susumu Kuno. 1975. The position of relative clauses and conjunctions. *Linguistic Inquiry,* 5(1):117-136.

Roland W. Langacker. 2008. *Cognitive Grammar: A Basic Introduction.* Oxford University Press, New York.

Roger Levy and Edward Gibson. 2013. Surprisal, the PDC, and the primary locus of processing difficulty in relative clauses. *Frontiers in Language Sciences,* 4:229.

Brian MacWhinney. 2008. A Unified Model. In N. Ellis & P. Robinson (eds.), *Handbook of Cognitive Linguistics and Second Language Acquisition*, pp. 341-372. Lawrence Erlbaum Press, New York.

Brian MacWhinney. 2013. The logic of the Unified Model. In S. Gass & A. Mackey (eds.), *Handbook of Second Language Acquisition*, pp. 211–227. Routledge, New York.

William O'Grady. 2005. *Syntactic Carpentry: An Emergentist Approach to Syntax.* Erlbaum, Mahwah, NJ.

Hannah Rohde, Roger Levy and A. Kehler. 2011. Anticipating explanations in relative clause processing. *Cognition,* 118(3):339-358.

Günter Rohdenburg. 2003. Cognitive complexity and horror aequi as factors determining the use of interrogative clause linkers in English. In G. Rohdenburg and B. Mondorf (eds.), *Determinants of grammatical variation in English*, pp. 205-249. Mouton de Gruyter. Berlin.

Dan I. Slobin. 1973. Cognitive prerequisites for the development of grammar. In Charles A. Ferguson and Dan Slobin (eds.), *Studies of Child Language Development*, pp. 175-208. Holt, Rinehart & Winston, New York.

Amy Sheldon. 1974. The role of parallel function in the acquisition of relative clauses in English. *Journal of Verbal Learning and Verbal Behavior*, 13:272-281.

Strasser H, Weber C (1999). On the Asymptotic Theory of Permutation Statistics. *Mathematical Methods of Statistics*, 8:220250.

Caroline Strobl, Anne-Laure Boulesteix, Thomas Kneib, Thomas Augustin and Achim Zeileis. 2008. Conditional variable importance for random forests. *BMC Bioinformatics,* 9:307.

Caroline Strobl, James Malley and Gerhard Tutz. 2009. An introduction to recursive partitioning: Rationale, application and characteristics of classification and regression trees, bagging and random forests. *Psychological Methods,* 14(4):323-348.

Michael Tomasello. 2003. *Constructing a Language: A Usage-Based Theory of Language Acquisition.* Harvard University Press, Harvard.

Marjolijn Verspoor, Monika S. Schmid & Xiaoyan Xu. 2012. A dynamic usage-based perspective on L2 writing. *Journal of Second Language Writing,* 21(3):239-263.

Daniel Wiechmann. 2010. *Understanding Complex Constructions: A Quantitative Corpus-Linguistic Approach to the Processing of English Relative Clauses*. PhD Thesis. University of Jena.

Daniel Wiechmann & Elma Kerz. 2014. Cue reliance in L2 written production. *Language Learning*.

Daniel Wiechmann, Elma Kerz, Neal Snider & T. Florian Jaeger. 2013. Special issue: Parsimony and Redundancy in Models of Language. *Language and Speech,* 56(3).

Willem Zuidema. 2006. What are the productive units of natural language grammar? A DOP approach to the automatic identification of constructions. *Proceedings CoNLL* 2006, 29–36.

Author Index

Araujo, Márcio José, 3

Bel Enguix, Gemma, 43
Bentz, Christian, 38
Blache, Philippe, 1
Blasi, Helena Ferro, 3
Bungum, Lars, 49
Buttery, Paula, 38

Cimiano, Philipp, 30
Clark, Alexander, 29
Çöltekin, Çağrı, 19

Frank, Stella, 14

Gambäck, Björn, 49
Gaspers, Judith, 30

Kerz, Elma, 55

Lekvam, Torvald, 49
Lemme, Andre, 30

Nerbonne, John, 19

Panzner, Maximilian, 30
Pearl, Lisa, 9
Phillips, Lawrence, 9

Rapp, Reinhard, 43
Rohlfing, Katharina J., 30

Vasilévski, Vera, 3

Wiechmann, Daniel, 55
Wrede, Sebastian, 30

Zock, Michael, 43